When LAMBS Become LIONS

CONNIE ZENO

Copyright © 2023 Connie Zeno.

All rights reserved. No part of this book may be reproduced, stored, or transmitted by any means—whether auditory, graphic, mechanical, or electronic—without written permission of both publisher and author, except in the case of brief excerpts used in critical articles and reviews. Unauthorized reproduction of any part of this work is illegal and is punishable by law.

ISBN: 979-8-88640-854-6 (sc)
ISBN: 979-8-88640-855-3 (hc)
ISBN: 979-8-88640-856-0 (e)

Because of the dynamic nature of the Internet, any web addresses or links contained in this book may have changed since publication and may no longer be valid. The views expressed in this work are solely those of the author and do not necessarily reflect the views of the publisher, and the publisher hereby disclaims any responsibility for them.

One Galleria Blvd., Suite 1900, Metairie, LA 70001
1-888-421-2397

CONTENTS

Foreword v

Acknowledgements vii

Introduction ix

Chapter 1   We Are Loaded and Don't Know It 1

Chapter 2   Say It Ain't So 43

Chapter 3   If You Ain't Praying 63

Chapter 4   When Lambs Become Lions 71

References 79

FOREWORD

Dear Reader,

Are you as excited as I am when I consider the possibility that *"Lambs Can Become Lions"*? In the natural, these two animals don't have the same DNA. In fact, they are diametrically opposed in personality, attitude, and action. Certainly, they are on opposite ends of the dietary chain. Suffice it to say, changing from a lamb to a lion is not a "skin" change but a total transformation.

I want to make it clear that I'm not criticizing God's creation, lambs and lions, or saying that one has more importance than the other. But when it comes to the subject of living an overcoming life, lambs take flight and lions fight.

Connie gives us important instruction and tools to live an overcoming life. Who wouldn't want that? The choice is <u>to</u> overcome or <u>be</u> overcome. I know what choice I want to make.

Only the Creator, God, can alter the created. As you read this book, put yourself in the hands of God to be transformed. You may have begun as a lamb, but you can finish as a lion. Remember, we do have an adversary (1 Pet. 5:8) who is a lion that devours sheep; but lions fight lions. It is time to rise up!

It was very encouraging to see Connie's inspiration for this book from the words inscribed on the handle of a sword. The Bible tells us that the sword is symbolic of the Word of God (Eph. 6:17). So, if we take the sword in hand, it will transform us by the inscription therein. Connie quotes the Word continually, which gives this book its authority. She writes with inspiration, as well as revelation.

Enjoy your journey through this book, and as you approach the last chapter, your transformation is already on its way. In fact, once you are finished reading, you might want to look in the mirror. Behold, the face of a lion!

Apostle David Cunningham

Rancho Christian Center

Rancho Cucamonga, California

ACKNOWLEDGEMENTS

First of all I want to give thanks and praise to my Lord and Savior, Jesus. This book was written by His inspiration. Thank you, Lord for a renewed fire in my heart. Thank you, Father, for your precious Holy Spirit and thank you Father for your persistent nudging me to finish this project.

I want to thank my apostle Dave Cunningham for his counsel and wisdom. You honored me in agreeing to write the forward to this book. Zee and I greatly appreciate yours and Vivian's friendship.

I want to thank our pastoral staff, Jim and Donna Weston for encouraging words and honoring that you displayed towards my family and the family of God. Pastor's Jim and Donna, you both have such a heart of love. It gushes out from you both. I am certainly blessed to know you.

To my family and friends thank you for your support. It has meant the world to me. I have been blessed with a wonderful husband. Zee, you have been a continual source of encouragement. I love you.

Connie Zeno

INTRODUCTION

One Friday afternoon, my husband and I went to the movies to see *Robin Hood* starring Russell Crowe as Robin Hood. In one of the scenes, Robin is entrusted with a fellow countryman's sword as the man lay dying after a battle. The dying man's request was for Robin to go to his homeland and tell his father of his death. When Robin agrees to this arrangement, the man dies. Later, on the voyage back to England, Robin notices writing on the handle of the sword. He begins to peel away the covering. And in doing so, these words are revealed—"Rise and rise again until" on one side and on the other side, "lambs become lions." As I sat there viewing the movie, I could not stop thinking about those words "Rise and rise again until lambs become lions" the more I contemplated the more I felt compelled to write this book.

The Body of Christ is identified in a variety of ways by our Lord, but none as persistent as our identification as "lambs." Jesus was called the Lamb of God. *After Jesus' accession, it was now the third time that Jesus revealed Himself to the disciples. After they had eaten Jesus asked Simeon Peter "Do you love Me?" Simeon said to Him "Yes Lord. You know that I love You." Jesus said "Feed My lambs." Again He asked him the second time, "Do you love Me?" Simeon said to Him, "Yes Lord, You know that I love you." Jesus said to him "Shepherd tend My sheep." He said to him the third time, "Simeon, do you love Me?" Even though Peter was grieved that He should ask him the third time, do you love Me, he said to Jesus,* "Lord You know everything. You know that I love You." *Jesus said to him,* "Feed My sheep." By commandment from God lambs have been used in sacrificial ceremonies for the atonement of sin. I have always been fascinated with the Lord's comparison of believers to lambs. Lambs are docile creatures. They are easily led astray. They pose no threat to other animals. They love to be in groups. They are dependent upon their shepherd for protection and direction. They don't appear to be conscious of present danger. Sheep are also extremely food oriented. Sheep have many wants, yet they are very helpless and quite unable to provide for themselves. But for the shepherd's cure, they would soon perish. This also is our case. Our spiritual needs are numerous and pressing yet we cannot supply any of them. (Spurgeon, The Sheep and Their Shepherd)

> *"All we like sheep have gone astray?"*
> Isaiah 53:6

We have this remarkable tendency to believe God and follow after Him, but we soon stray away from Him and find ourselves in other pastures. We have no sense of impending danger while grazing on luscious food. We quickly discover that we have wandered off the path and now are in need of rescue. Our Shepherd saves us from danger and places us back in the safety zone. We are a forgetful group too. Our memory banks don't seem to recall the incalculable incidences where the hand of the Lord protected us or deflected harm from us. We at times are remotely aware of the land mines, ditches and booby traps the enemy has set for us. But in His love and grace He spares us from many of the enemy's traps. We can find ourselves ensnared by the trappings of the enemy, our flesh, and the world because we take our focus off our Shepherd and venture down paths that the Lord never destined for us to walk.

> *"The Lord is my Shepherd, I shall not want. He leads me down paths of righteousness for His name's sake."*
> Psalm 23:1, 3

Notice the word *path* is plural. There are many paths where He will lead His people. The paths that He chooses for us will always work for our good. His plan for us is good and awesome with hope for a promising future. But He is the one leading and not we ourselves. Our responsibility is to hear the Master's voice and obey Him. Sounds so simple, and yet as sheep, we have a tendency to complicate even the simplest of assignments. We love grazing on the various delicacies of theology, new teachings, and fresh revelations from heaven while ignoring present dangers. Sheep are totally dependent on the shepherd for everything. Like our natural examples, we are called to be totally dependent on our Shepherd, Jesus. He is our Protector. He is our Provider. He is our Healer. He is our Salvation. We can rest assured that whatever we need, whatever we lack, Jesus is the answer. We are in Him. *In Him we also were made God's heritage and we obtained an inheritance; for we had been chosen and appointed beforehand in accordance with His purpose, Who works out everything in agreement with the counsel and design of His will. (Ephesians 1:11 amplified)* He is the Author and Finisher of our faith. Therefore, our confidence is not in what we can do but is in who He is and what He can do in us and through us and in most cases, in spite of us.

Beloved we were made for such a time as this. The Scriptures identifies the Church as glorious and how the Church will advance the kingdom of God on earth.

Jesus prayed, *"Our Father in heaven, hallowed is Your name. Your kingdom come. Your will be done, on earth as it is in heaven." Matthew 6:9,10*

It is our responsibility as God's ambassadors to make the will of God a reality in the earth today. We are in a time now where the glory of the latter house shall be greater than the glory former house. In order for our house to be the conquering, overcoming, setting-the-captives-free house, we must become lions whose leader is the Lion of the tribe of Judah. The time and season of being sheep that are afraid of their own shadow, who cringe at the thought of being attacked, who the world sees as insignificant, powerless, and voiceless—those times are over!

We must arise out of the muck and mire of religion and discard those dead man clothes. There is a new day dawning, where the sons of God are coming forth.

> *"Arise, shine; for thy light has come! And the glory of the Lord is risen upon you."* Isaiah 60:1

The whole earth has been waiting for the sons of God to rise up and take their righteous place. There are nations waiting for us to be the true sons and daughters of God. The clock is ticking, and time is running out. This message is an end-time message to and for an end-time people. It's time, beloved, for the lambs to become lions. We are called to be transformers and world changers. It was said of the early church, these are they who have turned the world upside down. Will the same be said of you and me?

As for me, I want to be a history maker in my generation. I don't want anything that I'm supposed to do be left undone. I want my Father's will done in the earth just like it is in heaven. The devil realizes his time is short, and he is pulling out all the stops. But God has a timetable for the earth, and we are approaching critical mass. God will have a people in the earth whose hearts beat for Him—a people who are willing to live for God no matter what, a people who know their God and will do great exploits for His kingdom. We are that people, and the time is now.

When we grasp the revelation of us being more lion like than as lambs, we will seize the day. Saints we are living on borrowed time. The time of watching our society decay while we do little to stop it has passed. The Lord is calling His Church to rise up from her slumber and be the head and not the tail. No longer a silent majority but ones that will roar with a mighty roar against the works of darkness. When lambs become lions, no family is untouched, no nation is unchanged, and no society is unaffected. The Lord is calling His people. Will you answer the call?

*Why do we act as though we
are a people with no hope in this world?*

CHAPTER 1

WE ARE LOADED AND DON'T KNOW IT

Have you ever read the Bible and wondered why your life does not match up with the people you are reading about? Doesn't it appear that those in the Bible had more advantages than we, excluding the technological advances of course? Good news, saints, if God did miracles for the nation of Israel, He will do them for the Body of Christ too. Jesus demonstrated to everyone how the kingdom of God operates. We are privileged and authorized by the Son to operate in the kingdom the way He did. He did nothing except what He saw the Father do. He said nothing except what He heard the Father say. His will was to do the Father's will all the time, even when it meant going to the cross.

So, what has been the problem with the Body of Christ not walking in the fullness of her destiny? I believe we have been living under erroneous narratives. I will address what is in my heart. This by no means is an all-inclusive list. Having ministered to people over the last fifteen plus years, these are the ones we consistently see. They are the following:

(1) A narrative that says we just need to endure until we lay this tired old body down and transfer to heaven then it will all be worth it. All the misery, all the unhappiness, all the defeats, all the pains, all the sufferings are part of our little hapless lives as born-again believers.

(2) Or what about this narrative, in order for you to be holy, you must be poor because being poor is equal to humility. Therefore, the thought of being prosperous has been a foreign concept to the church.

(3) Or the narrative that says you can be seen but not heard. But if you must speak, you cannot use the Bible as your foundation because after all, times have changed, and the Bible is no longer relevant, and absolutely do not use the name of Jesus in advancing the kingdom of God.

(4) Or my favorite narrative, we are born-again believers, but we don't believe anything good will happen to and for us. We are adept at believing the bad and negative reports from sources other than the Lord Himself.

(5) And the granddaddy of them all, a narrative that says all power was given to Jesus, but His church has to limp along powerless, ineffective, and inefficient and fearful of a defeated foe.

We have the greatest success story ever written. We have a proven track record. We should be exclaiming every day the marvelous works of the Lord. Instead, we have believed false narratives of what someone else says about who we are and what we can and cannot do. Let us take a moment to look at each of these narratives in view of scripture.

(1) We just need to endure until we lay this tired old body down:

The idea that the Body of Christ must endure sufferings to the extent that we assume an inferior posture in the earth is religious in its origin.

> *"We are bound to thank God always for you, brethren, as it is fitting, because your faith grows exceedingly, and the love of every one of you all abounds towards each other, so that we ourselves boast of you among the churches of God for your patience and faith in all your persecutions and tribulations that you endure, which is manifest evidence of the righteous judgment of God, that you may be counted worthy of the kingdom of God, for which you also suffer."*
> 1 Thessalonians 1:3–5

> *"For I consider that the sufferings of this present time are not worthy to be compared with the glory which shall be revealed in us."* Romans 8:18

> *"Beloved, do not think it strange concerning the fiery trial which is to try you, as though some strange thing happened to you; but rejoice to the extent that you partake of Christ's sufferings, that when His glory is revealed you may also be glad with exceeding joy."* 1 Peter 4:12–13

Endurance for the believer is like a long-distance race. The race is long, and it will test your stamina and endurance. It will reveal the results of your training, whether it was beneficial or not. We are born into this world, and we're supposed to run our race well to the very end. Jesus did not go to the cross for us so that when we get saved, we spend our lives wishing and hoping for the rapture. This theology of suffering actually comes out of the Dark Ages.

The Dark Ages historically was from the fall of Rome (AD 476) to the fall of Constantinople (AD 1453). The period of the Dark Ages for the spiritual church was from its deterioration into an apostate condition in the fifth century until the beginning of its restoration in the fifteenth century. Culturally it was from the time when the civilized world was overrun by uneducated "barbarians" in the fifth century until the beginning of the Renaissance in the fifteenth century. During this time, the church not only deteriorated doctrinally but degenerated morally as well. The twenty-two-year period just prior to, and a little after, the year 1000 is called by historians the *Midnight of the Dark Ages*. There was little justice and mercy in the world. The Christian Church was reduced to an empty form with virtually no life, love, or hope to offer suffering humanity (Hamon, *The Eternal Church*).

The Dark Ages was the epitome of suffering. We have carried this idea of suffering for the Lord down through the ages. The Bible says that we shall be persecuted for our faith in Christ Jesus, but it does not say that persecution comes from God. Ultimately, persecution derives its origin from the devil himself, who uses people to carry out his diabolical works. When God created man He gave man authority and dominance over the earth. He was commanded to subdue it, keep it and rule it.

When Adam sinned against God everything changed. Satan used the method of suggestion on Adam and Eve. Before submitting to the thought, they could have used their authority to quell Satan's tactic. Sadly, they did not. Man, now a fallen being with a fallen nature, is susceptible to the thoughts and plans of the enemy. Yes, we are to suffer for Christ; but it is not what religion has purported it to be.

Suffering for Christ is not sickness and disease. Jesus bore our sickness and diseases on His body. We have been redeemed from sin, sickness and death. And yet organized religion has told people that God put sickness on people to teach them something. Faced with the possibility of fighting against God or accepting His will folks usually opted to accept the sickness and suffer through it because they were told it was their cross to bear. From a historical perspective, the early Church operated from a *warfare world view*. This was the predominate understanding for about 500 years. Within this worldview, believers were to fight against sickness, disease and demonic oppression through the power of the Holy Spirit. This warfare caused the sickness and demonic bondages people experienced. The change in mindset occurred when Augustine, a leader in the western Roman Catholic Church, writings influenced the western church. Augustine's writings moved the Church to a blueprint worldview. This view states that everything in life happens due to the predetermined will of God. This caused a shift in the thinking of the Church regarding healing. Now instead of believing that sickness was brought on by the devil, people believed that God brought on sickness for a person's spiritual sanctification. Therefore, to pray against an illness could be viewed as resisting God. (Johnson& Clark, The Essential Guide to Healing). This gave birth to erroneous preaching and teaching, that God put sickness on people for a variety of reason. Praise the Lord, the blueprint worldview is losing ground in the Body of Christ.

> *How God anointed Jesus of Nazareth with the Holy Spirit and with power, who went about doing good and healing all who were oppressed by the devil, for God was with Him. Acts 10:38*

What is the suffering that we are to endure? Suffering and persecution are not the same. Suffering is one of the most difficult things to understand in life and in Christianity. We know that God is good, and we know that He sees everything and is all-powerful. God does not delight in our suffering, but He is honored and pleased when we endure it with a good attitude. Trust requires unanswered questions. If we knew all the answers, faith would not even be necessary. Some people become angry at God when tragedy or extreme difficulty comes their way. This is the worst thing anyone can do because He is the only one who can help us.

God gave His only Son and allowed Him to go through unspeakable suffering that He did not deserve, and He did it for us. There are times when we go through things that God intends to use for our good and the good of others later in our lives. The test of faith is how we behave during trials and tribulations, especially ones we feel are totally unfair. Peter said that fiery ordeals and trials will come to test the quality of our faith and that we are *not to be amazed and bewildered. Instead, rejoice.* That right there is a trial, right? The last thing in the world I want to do is rejoice when I'm going through something. But in God's kingdom, we are supposed to do the opposite of what the world does. You see, our initial response to a trial, ordeal, or tragedy is shock, disbelief, and anger. Not faith or joy. So why has the Lord instructed us to count it all in joy? I believe, as we respond in a spiritual way, we allow the force and fruit of joy to carry us through. In everything we do in this life, we should come or respond in the opposite spirit. Is it challenging? Absolutely. It will require a retraining of our soul and flesh. I am not saying that we should walk around like robots, void of emotions. But at the end of the day, our emotions cannot and should not rule. Our emotions should not lead the way, and the same holds true for our minds, especially unrenewed minds.

> *"Consider it wholly joyful, my brethren, whenever you are enveloped in or encounter trials of any sort or fall into various temptations. Be assured and understand that the trial and proving of your faith bring out endurance and*

> *steadfastness and patience. But let patience have full play and do a thorough work, so that you may be people perfectly and fully developed with no defects, lacking in nothing."*
> *James 1:2-4 Amplified*

Nothing is wasted. God uses everything in our lives to bring us to a place of Christ likeness. Mind you, God is not the cause of the trial, but He sure gets blamed for much of it. We need to in love speak the truth to people. And stop telling folks that God took their baby or their loved one because He was lonely in heaven. Many times, ministers/pastors and well-meaning Christians say dumb things like that. Instead of comforting the person or family, they are guilty of accusing God. If you want to point the finger of accusation, point it at the devil. He is the one who steals, kills, and destroys. Not God. God poured out His wrath on Jesus as He hung on the cross. He is not mad at you. What the Lord has for us is only good. God is a good God.

I believe much of the suffering of believers in the western hemisphere, particularly in America, is a matter of surrender and submission to the will and plans of God. Our culture relishes independence, which is fine for a nation. Problems surface when people get saved having that mind-set and trying to operate in the same way in God's kingdom. In God's kingdom, self is not seated on the throne of our hearts. There is room for one, the Lord Himself. The Kingdom of God is a theocracy, a kingdom, with a King. We live by His rules. This is not a republic where the majority rule. One Lord, One King, One Word. Our mind requires renewing—a renewing or a brainwashing from a worldly perspective to a godly perspective.

We learn that we no longer are alive unto our selves but alive unto Christ. We have been purchased with the precious blood of Jesus, and our lives are not our own. Therefore, whatever plans we had for our future now belongs to the King of Kings.

> *"So, since Christ suffered in the flesh for us, for you, arm yourselves with the same thought and purpose. For whoever has suffered in the flesh is done with sin has stopped pleasing himself and the world and pleases God."* 1 Peter 4:1

Spiritual maturity or Christ likeness cannot be obtained without dying to self, which simply means saying yes to God and no to our flesh when our will and God's will are in opposition. *Not my will be done, but thy will be done,* said Jesus.

One of the main qualities of the Christian life is the ability to endure trouble, persecutions, and tribulations. The meaning of endure in the Greek is *"anechomai,"* which comes *from ana ("up") and echo ("to hold oneself up against").* The word carries the idea of persevering, tolerating, bearing with, putting up with, standing firm, and <u>not losing courage under pressure</u>. When a person accepts Jesus Christ into their lives, this does not mean that all their problems will automatically go away. God, through the power of the Holy Spirit, wants to teach us to triumph through endurance or staying power. Jesus wants us to go the distance in His power! Similar to a long distance runner, there are peaks and valleys along the way but he continues to run the race. There are unforeseen obstacles along the way but the runner continues to run. We are running a race and the Father's heart is for His people to finish their appointed races. We are to finish strong and well. We are not the image that religion portrays. A people barely making it across the finish line, battered and tattered hoping to make heaven their home. This certainly is not finale the Bible declares.

The Western church has no real concept of what real suffering is. What we call suffering is really inconvenience. We actually think suffering is being negatively talked about or the society in which we live maligning Christians or certain freedoms that we once enjoyed taken away or being singled out because of our beliefs. Jesus did not die for a wimpy, whiny, can't-take-a-punch Church.

Scripture says, *"I can do all things through Christ who strengthens me."*

Either the Word is true or it isn't. You'll never know until you put it to the test by using it. If you really, really, really want to know what true suffering is, go to China or to some of the Muslim nations where Christians are killed for their belief in Jesus. And yet, by the thousands, many are still making decisions for Christ, knowing fully what the cost might be. In the days of the early church, every prospective convert was advised of all the possible and probable things that may happen to them because of their conversion. And yet decisions for Christ were made. These decisions were not made lightly or with reservation but with the full understanding that it could literally cost them their lives. And for many it did. They did not lose courage while under pressure. I believe it would behoove every Christian to read *Foxe's Book of Martyrs*. You will gain an appreciation and respect for those who endured many cruel persecutions including death, while holding on to their faith in Jesus Christ. This was true for the young and old, men and women, poor and wealthy. Frankly, those who endured persecutions did not think themselves worthy to be named with our Lord and His sufferings. So, the next time you are tempted to say, "I'm suffering for the Lord," think again, my friend. Think about what real suffering looks like before you don the moniker of "I'm suffering for the Lord."

We must learn what it means to be authentic Christians. We must learn how to surrender all to Him and learn how to serve Him while living in our physical bodies. We must exchange our way of thinking and our way of doing for His way of thinking and doing. Beginning the lifetime journey of working out our salvation is an adventure. We have a new identity, a new name, and a new perspective on things.

> *"Therefore, if anyone is in Christ, he is a new creation; old things have passed away; behold, all things have become new."* 2 Corinthians 5:17

"The word new, kainos: means unused, fresh, novel. The word kainos means 'new' in regard to form and quality, rather than in reference to time, a thought conveyed by neos. It is one of the most wonderful and transforming truths in the Bible that for everyone who has ever wanted the chance to start all over again in life Jesus Christ gives them that opportunity" (Word Wealth, Spirit-Filled Life Bible).

"For if we have been united together in the likeness of his death, certainly we also shall be in the likeness of his resurrection. Knowing this, that our old man was crucified with him that the body of sin might be done away with that we should no longer be slaves of sin. For he who has died has been freed from sin. Now if we died with Christ, we believe that we shall also live with him. Therefore, do not let sin reign in your mortal body, that you should obey it in its lust. And do not present your members as instruments of unrighteousness to sin but present yourselves to God as being alive from the dead, and your members as instruments of righteousness to God for sin shall not have dominion you over you for you are not under the law but under grace." (Romans 6:5–8, 12–14 Spirit-Filled Life Bible)

Once you accept Jesus Christ into your life through faith, a basic reality goes to work: your old nature dies and you die spiritually to sin, and you become alive in Christ. Since you are spiritually dead to sin, sin should no longer have dominion over you. However, even though it is a spiritual reality that you are dead to sin, moment by moment, you must activate that reality through faith. In other words, moment by moment, you must choose with your will to reckon yourself dead to sin. This means by faith you have to choose to be dead to those things in your life that are displeasing to God. God has provided an abundance of grace for us to use in overcoming wrong behaviors, correcting bad habits, and changing mind-sets. *"My grace is sufficient for you."* Whatever the need, the problem, the situation—God's grace is sufficient to see us through.

This narrative of suffering the Body of Christ has operated under for generations must be changed. We can no longer afford to operate in this manner because time is winding down, and we must be about our father's business. *Jesus said, "I have come to give you life and to give you that life more abundantly."* As joint heirs with Jesus Christ, we must exercise our God-given authority to rule and reign in this life, just like Jesus ruled and reigned when He walked the earth. We must awaken unto righteousness and be the glorious church the Lord has called us to be. We are called to be holy, righteous, victorious, and to have abundance in every area of life. If Jesus is the head of the Church, and He is, all things have been put under his feet. We are His Body therefore, all things are put under our feet too. God is waiting for us to **be** the people of God that He has called us to be.

We must change our collective mind-sets from awaiting the rapture to one of being partners with God in ushering in His kingdom here on the earth. There is still much work to be done. There are billions of people on the continent of Asia that need to hear the gospel of Jesus Christ. There are millions of people that are living under yokes of bondage to religion and pagan worship that need to hear the gospel of Jesus Christ. And there are millions more who have never heard the gospel preached. It is the church's responsibility to proclaim with all boldness and confidence that there is only one true God and there is only one way to heaven. And that way is through Jesus Christ, Lord of all.

> *Jesus said, "I am the Way, the Truth and the Life; No one comes to the Father except through Me." John 14:6*

Jesus identified Himself as "the Way, the Truth and the Life." In addition, He said that He is the only way to God. It was only through the death and resurrection of Christ that the wall of sin that blocked man from God was done away with. Therefore, it is only through faith in Him that people can be forgiven of their sins and find God (Word Wealth, *Spirit-Filled Life Bible*).

(2) The second narrative that must be changed in the church's mind-set is the idea that says, in order for you to be pious or holy, you must be poor.

That is so far from the truth. The Lord never intended for the Body of Christ to be poor. The scripture says that *the Lord takes pleasure in the prosperity of His servants.*

> *"Beloved I wish above all things that thou may prosper and be in health, even as thy soul prospers." 3 John 2*

Austerity is not equal to holiness. This is an erroneous teaching that the church has perpetuated for generations. And this too has its origin in the Dark Ages. But its ultimate origin is from the pit of hell. Actually, it is just the opposite. God has always provided abundantly for His people and He always will. He is the same God yesterday, the same God today, the same God forever. He changes not.

> *"And God is able to make all grace (every favor an earthly blessing) come to you in abundance, so that you may always and under all circumstances and whatever the need be self-sufficient possessing enough to require no aid or support and furnish in abundance for every good work and charitable donation. (2 Corinthians 9:8 Amplified Bible)*

Prosperity for the believer begins on the inside first. Your soul must be transformed from its old way of thinking. All mind-sets must be replaced with new mind-sets that agree with the Word of God. Soul prosperity is vital for every Christian. Everyone who comes into the kingdom of God enters in as damaged goods. Our souls have been assaulted from the moment of conception, and for some, the assault began generations before you were born. Just like we have faith for healing, we need faith for prosperity and everything else that has been promised to us. The Word of God revealed by the Holy Spirit is the only true means for transforming the human heart. Renewing the mind by the Word is a continuing process. Spiritual disciples devour God's Word because in it is the key to a more dynamic relationship with their living Lord and a greater availability to the Holy Spirit.

> *"So, then faith cometh by hearing, and by hearing the word of God."* Romans 10:17

Faith does not come by having heard the Word of God, but the literal meaning is a continual hearing and hearing and hearing and hearing of the Word of God. It is the hearing of the Word of God and the meditating of the Word of God that will change the mind of the individual. Once the Word gets into your heart, then you must act on the Word. We must stop saying things that are contrary to God's Word.

> *"I call heaven and earth as witnesses today against you set before you life and death, blessing and cursing; therefore choose life, that both you and your descendant's may live." Deuteronomy 30:19*

Speak the Word of God regarding prosperity over your life. Speak the Word of God regarding prosperity over your children's lives. Speak the Word of God regarding prosperity over your circumstances. God has promised that when He hears His Word returning to Him, He will not allow His Word to come back to the earth without producing in the lives of the people that sent his Word back to Him. In other words, when we pray God's Word, God has put a guarantee on His Word that His Word will come to pass in our lives. *"I am alert and active, watching over My Word to perform it."* Often we pray one thing and yet speak something totally opposite of what we have prayed for. When we do, we cancel out our prayer requests. Then we sit back and wonder why we're not getting our prayers answered, but it is because of the things that we are saying in our tents. And that word *tents* simply means what you are saying in your mind. What are you saying to other people? What are you saying in your homes?

Newsflash: God is everywhere. He's omnipresent, and there is nothing that we can say nor do that gets beyond His purview. Therefore, speak the Word, and you will have good success. Meditate on the Word, and you will have good success. Act on the Word, and you will have good success.

> The Word says, *"I beseech you therefore, brethren, by the mercies of God, that you present your bodies a living sacrifice, holy, acceptable to God, which is your reasonable service. And do not be conformed to this world, but be transformed by the renewing of your mind that you may prove what is that good and acceptable and perfect will of God." Romans 12:1–2*

The Message's translation of Romans 12:2 says, *"Don't become so well-adjusted to your culture that you fit into it without even thinking."* The word *culture* in this verse can be defined as the attitudes, the opinions, the beliefs, and the behavior patterns that are characteristic of the country or the society in which we live (Savelle, *The Favor of God*).

For years the Church had become so well adjusted to the culture fitting into it without remorse. Our lives so mirrored the world that the dividing lines became obscure. We are betrothed to Jesus but sleeping with the enemy. We had become in our day like Israel was in the time of her harlotry.

> *"For of old I have broken your yoke and burst your bonds; And you said, 'I will not transgress,' When on every high hill and under every green tree. You lay down, playing the harlot. Yet I had planted you a noble vine, a seed of highest quality. How then have you turned before Me into the degenerate plant of an alien vine? For though you wash yourself with lye, and use much soap, yet your iniquity is marked before Me, says the Lord God." Jeremiah 2:20-22*

God pursued Israel while she was committing spiritual adultery. Because God has such great love for Israel and for the Church, He is not willing to share our affections. *We shall love the Lord God with all our heart, soul and body.* The Church and Israel have looked in the wrong places for love and satisfaction in life. We have chased lovers other than God, but we have discovered that sin would not bring the satisfaction we hungered for. Only in God's love can we find the true satisfaction we crave. The great philosopher Blaise Pascal said that inside of every man and woman is a God shaped vacuum. In other words, there is an emptiness in every human heart that only God can fill. My brother had a dream a few years ago, he was hovering over the Grand Canyon. He saw a man with a wheel barrow rolling it up a mountain. It was filled with stuff. The man walked to the edge and emptied the contents. Then turned around to get more stuff to empty into the canyon. Then Keith heard the Lord say, "the heart of man is like the Grand Canyon. Man endeavors to fill it up with all kinds of things. Only God is big enough to fill the void in man's heart."

God does not want us conformed to this present world system and its values and false belief systems. The word *conformed* refers to conforming oneself to the outer fashion or outward appearance, accommodating oneself to a model or pattern. God does not want His people programmed by the world's values or systems. Old programs should be deleted while initiating new programs.

Our programming must come from the Word of God. Who we are as people should not be defined by music, movies, television, or the society at large but by what God says about us in His Word. We get our inner belief systems and identification from God's Word, which causes us to live as free and powerful people.

"As a man thinks it in his heart, so is he."

Ingrained in our mind is poverty thinking. It has been there for generations. Jesus wants to pour into us the new wine, but He is hindered because we still have the old wineskins. He said, *"Nor do they put new wine into old wineskins or else the wineskins break the wine is spilled, and the wineskins are ruined. But they put new wine into new wine skins and both are preserved." Matthew 9:17*

We must delete this narrative of poverty living. We must change from having a poverty mind-set to minds *set* on having an abundant prosperous life. We don't have to ink out our existence here on planet Earth, just waiting for the day when we go to heaven. What kind of Father is He? Heaven's streets are paved with gold while His children are barely having enough, living a meager existence, never quite having enough to support their families' type of life here on planet Earth? God does not say one thing and then does something totally different. Examine the scriptures, and you will find that God is consistent. God promised Abraham that He would bless him and his seed. The blessing included Abraham's spiritual seed. This is a perpetual blessing.

> *"If any man be in Christ then are you Abraham's seed."*
> *Galatians 3:29*

The Message's translation says, *"In Christ's family there can be no division into Jew and non-Jew, slave and free, male or female. Among us you are all equal. That is, we are all in a common relationship with Jesus Christ. Also since you are Christ's family, then you are Abraham's famous descendants, heirs according to the covenant promises."*

Question, who will finance the gospel of Jesus Christ if the Church won't and can't? Who will feed the poor if the Church won't and can't? Who will the world look to when the economy collapses? Who will send the missionaries to foreign lands to preach the gospel of Jesus Christ? If the Church is sitting back believing a false narrative that the church should be poor, that we should not ask God for anything or believe God for material things or will not believe God for finances, then who is going to do the work of the kingdom? So who will get the work of the kingdom done? Is it the world's responsibility to do so? Or are God's people responsible to do it? It's one or the other, not both. The Body of Christ has been commissioned to carry out the work of the kingdom.

Do you think Satan is going to get the work done? Absolutely not! He is the one hoarding the money and trying to keep it away from God's people. It is time for the Body of Christ to rise from her slumber and be the glorious, overcoming, abundant church that God has called us to be. But it will require us going in and taking back what rightfully belongs to us. *Jesus said that I have come to give you life and life more abundantly, to the full, till it overflows.* He did not say I have come to give you scarcity or to live as beggars who are impoverished, defeated, and victimized. It will require us to refute arguments, theology, doctrines, and traditions of men that are contrary to God's will.

> *The word "poor" means a beggar, having little or no money, goods, or other means of support, dependent on charity or public support, deficient or lacking in something specified, scanty, meager, or paltry in amount or number.*
>
> *The word "prosper" means to succeed in an enterprise or activity, especially to achieve economic success, to cause to succeed or thrive. Marked by success or economic well-being, enjoying vigorous and healthy growth, flourishing.*
>
> *The synonym for "prosper" is to flourish, increase, multiply, progress, advance, augment, benefit.*

Much of the church world has lived as beggars. The United States, the most affluent country on the planet, has within her the Church of the Lord Jesus Christ, many who are living and operating at levels far below what God desires for them. We need to see ourselves as God sees us. The Body of Christ must step into her destiny. There are over seven thousand promises in God's Word. Take the promises that address prosperity and finances and declare them over your life. Meditate on those scriptures until the Word becomes engrafted into your heart.

We are the spiritual seed of Abraham. God's promise to him was blessings. Our Father desires for His people to be blessed in every arena of life so that we in turn can be a blessing to others. It's challenging to bless someone else when you are struggling. God's blessings are not for us to squander on our lust. Yes, He wants our needs met; and when they are, we'll be able to turn our focus outward and bless others.

Prosperity is God's idea and not man's. We have been marked by God for success. *"For I know the thoughts that I think toward you, says the Lord, thoughts of peace and not of evil, to give you a future and a hope."* In the Garden of Eden, God commanded for the man to have dominion over all the Lord had made. He was instructed to go and multiply, dress it, keep it, and subdue it.

> *"Then God bless them and God said to them, be fruitful and multiply; fill the earth and subdue it; and have dominion over the fish of the sea, over the birds of the air, and over every living thing that moves on the earth."* Genesis 1:28 Spirit-Filled Life Bible

God's Word teaches us how to prosper. Of course, prosperity is not just about riches or material possessions. Real prosperity is total well-being in every area of life—spiritually, mentally, emotionally, physically, socially, and financially. The Bible never teaches that Christians should be poor. Over and over in the scriptures, we find that when a person walked upright before God, He blessed them and caused the works of their hands to prosper. Now is the time to *change* how you think and react when you hear certain words like *rich*, *wealthy*, *prosperity*, *money*, and *abundance*. Let the Word renew your mind. These words should not be foreign to the believer. When the Lord says He takes pleasure in the prosperity of His servants, we should be shouting, "Yes. Amen, Lord, that's me!"

When you read, *"And God is able to make all grace, every favor and earthly blessing come to you in abundance, so that you may always and under all circumstances and whatever the need, be self-sufficient, possessing enough to require no aid or support and furnished in abundance for every good work and charitable donation"* (2 Corinthians 9:8 Amplified), our response should be "I receive that. Thank You, Lord."

Your daily confession should be "Lord, I am a tither and giver. And because I am, thank You for supplying all my needs according to Your riches in glory in Christ Jesus, my Lord."

We have much to be thankful for. Our God has made everything available for us to live an abundant life right here, right now. Many believers are going to be shocked when they get to heaven and realize what they could have walked in and what they could have possessed while on the earth. There are things/stuff the Lord has set aside just for our use in this life. As for me and my house, we intend to use everything the Lord has made available for us now. I don't want to leave any leftovers. My brothers and sisters, if you don't know that something has been set aside for you, then you will not venture to ask the Father for it.

The Word says, *"You have not because you ask not. And when you ask, you ask amiss." James 4:3*

Meaning you don't ask for what you should ask for, and when you ask for something, you ask for the wrong thing. For example, I need a new car and I see sister Lillian with a new car, and I begin to covet sister Lillian's new car. So I go to the Lord, asking Him to give me sister Lillian's car. I cannot do that! That is coveting my neighbor's goods. I am asking amiss. What I can do is ask the Lord for a car of my own, something like what sister Lillian has. Now I have prayed a legal prayer.

Much too often, we have been taught that the Lord is holding out on us. In other words, He's holding things back from us. That is not entirely true. Sometimes it's a timing issue. Sometimes it's because we are not ready to receive (for one reason or another), but I believe much of the time, we simply have not asked the Lord in faith, believing we have received our petitions. Without faith, it is impossible to please God.

The very best investment a person can make is an investment in the kingdom of God. The Lord admonishes us to seek first His kingdom instead of worrying about material possessions.

> *"Seek first his kingdom and his righteousness, and all these things will be added to you." Matthew 6:33*

American Christians today have more resources available to them on a day-to-day basis than any previous generation. On the other hand, there has never been a generation of Christians so caught up in worry about possessions as this present-day generation is. However, it is not the material things that cause the difficulties; it is materialism, which is a heart attitude. Basically, materialism means that a person is more dedicated in accumulating material things than serving God. Without a doubt, the evidence of the lives of most Christians in America reveals this generation's dedication to materialism.

> *"For where your treasure is, there will your heart be also." Matthew 6:21*

We have grown complacent and comfortable with God's blessings and have forgotten Jesus' mandate. Since God ask for obedience rather than demanding it, many Christians have simply ignored the very reason for God's blessings, and that is to glorify Him and to honor His Word. We have enough money in North America to fund all the Christian work in the world—if the people of God would just give. But although the desire to give may be there, most Christians in America are so caught up in the acquisition of things, making money, and living a pseudo-Christian life that they have lost their focus on the unsaved world. Their debt has enslaved them to a system that was never designed to liberate them. In essence, the gospel has literally become shackled because money needed for worldwide ministry is tied up in personal debt and large monthly payments. We have taken this seeking the kingdom of God first and reversed it in our actions and in our mind by seeking our own kingdom first rather than seeking God's kingdom. We must get back to biblical order.

In many of our churches today, teaching about money, teaching about God's desire to prosper His people is discouraged by the denominational hierarchy. Jesus came to set the captives free, and yet people are still in bondage. They are in bondage to religion, they are in bondage to poverty, they are in bondage to wrong mind-sets, and they are in bondage to what other people think. What matters—the only thing that matters—is what God thinks and what God says in His Word.

Thank God for the men and women who believe the Word of God and preach and teach the Word concerning prosperity. These pioneers of faith received a lot of push back from ministers, Christians, and the world because of their lack of revelation about who God is. God is love. He doesn't have love. He is love. God demonstrated His love for mankind that He was not willing to let man be lost for all eternity. So He made a way of escape because, rightfully, we were all destined for hell because of the sin of Adam. We were shaped in iniquity and born into this world as sinful creatures.

But thanks be to God that He was not willing to let us remain that way. So God sent His only begotten son, Jesus the Christ, born in a manger, Savior of all mankind. God is a giver. And as His heirs, we are just like our Father, God. It's in our nature to give, but because our nature has been perverted by sin and has been corrupted by Satan himself, we have become self-centered and not God-centered. The requirement for redemption was the new birth.

After the new birth, our journey of learning a new way—having new ideals and new attitudes—began. God has always blessed His people, but His people have not always been in a position to receive His blessings. As the time on the hourglass winds down and the world continues to grow darker and darker with sin, the Body of Christ must step up to the plate and start swinging. We cannot afford to be spectators. We must start being the light of the world and begin illuminating in dark places. Our lamps are not lit to be placed under bushels. They are to be out in the open, dispelling darkness. We have been given everything by the Lord Jesus Christ to be successful on planet Earth. We must push back darkness and free those that are held captive, and we must go into all the byways and highways and to the uttermost parts of the earth, and that requires finances. It's time, my brothers and sisters, to shake off those dead man clothes. Discard dead theology and be kings and priests advancing the gospel of Jesus Christ like never before. Begin to believe God for your finances. Time to live the abundant and the full life Jesus declared in order to help finance the kingdom of God. So when God asks you to give, you won't be saying, "Lord, how can I give because I don't have anything." But your question will be "Where do you want me to give, God, and how much?" and not "I can't afford to."

For too long, the church has been saying "I can't." It's time for us to say, *"God will provide. I can do all things through Christ who strengthens me."*

(3) I want to address the last part of this narrative first. We are told by the society at large not to use the name of Jesus.

Brethren, this narrative is not a new one. This has been around since the apostle Peter walked the earth. He was told in his day that he could not use the name of Jesus by the religious order, the Pharisees and the Sadducees. They whipped him and threw him in jail before they released him. They ordered him not to speak in that name any longer.

> *"Now when they saw the boldness of Peter and John, and perceived that they were uneducated and untrained men, they marveled. And they realized that they had been with Jesus. And, seeing the man who had been healed standing with them, they could say nothing against. But when they*

had commanded them to go aside out of the counsel, they conferred among themselves, saying, what shall we do to these men? For indeed that a notable miracle has been done through them is evident to all who dwell in Jerusalem, and we cannot deny it. But so that it spreads no further among the people, let us severely threaten them, that from now on they speak to no man in this name. So they called them and commanded them not to speak at all nor teach in the name of Jesus. But Peter and John answered and said to them, whether it is right in the sight of God to listen to you more than to God, you judge. For we cannot but speak the things which we have seen and heard. So when they had further threatened them, they let them go, finding no way of punishing them because of the people, since they all glorified God for what had been done." Acts 4:13–21

I love the boldness of Peter and John. The religious leaders perceived that they were unlearned and untrained men. They took note that these men had been with Jesus. They recognized the anointing on Peter and John because they witnessed the same anointing on Jesus. Fear filled them enough that they commanded them not to teach or speak in the name of Jesus.

Ever since Jesus defeated Satan in hell, Satan has sought to stop man from using the name of Jesus. The Bible says that *at that name of Jesus, every knee bows and every tongue confesses that Jesus Christ is Lord of all.* Satan understands this, so he endeavors to persecute, deceive, use fear tactics, and whatever will work against Christians from rightfully using the name of Jesus. The world uses His name, but they use His name in a profane way. But we use His name because His name is holy. His name is above every name that is named. In His name, there is healing. And in His name, there is salvation. And in His name there is freedom, there is deliverance, and there is victory and so much more. And also, His name reminds the devil of his defeat. And he knows that there is power, wonder-working power in the precious, magnificent, marvelous, and matchless name of Jesus. Therefore, he works overtime to persecute those who are called by His name. He uses the world to come against Christians, mocking us and shaming us into not using His name. But oh, my friend, the telling part about this whole thing is, if the name of Jesus was ineffective, then why is the devil fighting so hard to discourage believers from using His name? If the name of Jesus had no authority, there would not be a fight. If the name of Jesus was not endued with power, then why is the devil spending time and resources to defame our Lord's name?

It's funny that we don't see the same type of struggle in the world when someone uses Confucius's name or Buddha's name or Muhammad's name—because Confucius, Buddha, and Muhammad were just mere men. They were not the Son of God come in the flesh. They did not die for all mankind. God did not confer on them a name above all names.

When Jesus hung on the cross, the devil and his cohorts thought they had the victory. But after three days and three nights in hell, divine justice was satisfied, and God said, "Enough!" Jesus rose up and took the keys of death, hell, and the grave from Satan. Here's what scripture says, *"Having wiped out the handwriting of requirements that was against us, which was contrary to us. And He has taken it out of the way having nailed it to the cross. Having disarmed principalities and powers, He made a public spectacle of them, triumphing over them in it." Colossians 2: 14–15*

> *"But we speak the wisdom of God in a mystery, the hidden wisdom which God ordained before the ages for our glory, which none of the rulers of this age knew for had they known, they would not have crucified the Lord of glory."*
> *1 Corinthians 2:7–8*

We have been given the name of Jesus through covenant. When we accept Jesus as our personal Lord and Savior, there is a name exchange. He gives us His name. Jesus said to the disciples, "Ask the Father in My name, and He will give it to you."

The Father has exalted the name of Jesus above every name that is named. The name of Jesus has power in heaven, on earth and under the earth, in the seen and the unseen realm. No wonder the devil fights the believer from using His name. Up to this point, Satan has been successful in removing Jesus' name from the normal discourse among people. He has strategized and twisted statements from our founding fathers to promote a separation of church and state mantra. Frankly, our Constitution and the writings of our founding fathers indicate the opposite. They believed in the providence of God and that our nation should inquire and seek the guidance of the Almighty. However, if you tell a lie long enough, people will think it to be true. The devil has even convinced people to use Jesus' name as a curse word. There is a rampant dishonoring of our Lord's name. And some of the dishonoring is coming from Christians. When you say Jesus' name in a defaming way, you dishonor Him. Example, you kick your toe and you say, "Jesus Christ."

We are to purposely use His name when we transact business in the kingdom and for the kingdom of God. Uses like the example above are defaming His name or using the Lord's name in vain. As believers, this speaks to the issue of renewing our minds. We are not like the world. We cannot say what they say. We cannot do what they do. We have been redeemed from all that. Jesus' name is to be honored and revered.

> *"There is no other name given under heaven given among men by which we shall be saved." Acts 4:12*

> *"Therefore God has also highly exalted Him and given Him the name which is above every name, that at the name of Jesus every knee should bow, of those in heaven, and those on earth, and those under the earth, and that every tongue should confess that Jesus Christ is Lord, to the glory of God the Father." Philippians 2:9–11*

We used to sing a song that says,

> "Jesus, Jesus, Jesus
> There's just something about that name
> Master, Savior, Jesus
> Like the fragrance after the rain
> Jesus, Jesus, Jesus
> Let all heaven and earth proclaim
> Kings and kingdoms shall all pass away
> But there's something about that name."
> By Bill Gaither/Gloria Gaither

The name of Jesus moves the hand of God. The name of Jesus causes the demons to tremble. The name of Jesus is beloved by those called by His name. So, beloved, do not shy away from using our Lord's name to advance the kingdom of God. He died for us to freely use His name. We honor Him when we rely on His name. For God so loved the world that He gave us His son and all that comes with His son. There is power, wonder-working power, in the precious name of Jesus.

Now let us look at the next narrative the Body of Christ is confronted with today. The narrative that says you can be seen but not heard. But if you must speak, you cannot use the Bible as your foundation because, after all, times have changed and the Bible is no longer relevant.

The foundation of Jesus Christ's church is the Word of God. *"If the foundations are destroyed, what can the righteous do?" Psalm 11:4*

> *"In the beginning was the Word and the Word was with God and the Word was God." John 1:1*

There has been a consistent denigration from society attempting to render the Bible irrelevant. However, within the populace, there is a collection of people that love God and love His Word. Societies change, empires come and go, but the Word of the Lord never changes.

> *"My covenant I will not break, nor alter the word that has gone out of My lips." Psalm 89:34*

How different is the twenty-first century from the first-century church? If we could take a cursory glance at the first- and twenty-first-century churches, we would see stark differences as well as similarities. As I read the book of Acts and other accounts of the first-century church, what is indicative is their unity, their genuine hunger for God, and how they searched the scriptures, verifying what the apostles preached. Scripture says that God worked with them, confirming His Word with signs following. The twenty-first-century church is encumbered with many distractions. We have allowed our faith to drift and our passion for the Lord to become lukewarm. Our reliance on Him, on His Word, has been replaced by secular opinions and schemes.

The Bible contains the Old and New Testament. The Old Testament points to the cross, and the New Testament points back to the cross. The Bible has remained atop of the best-seller list of all time. Another word for *testament* is *covenant*. God outlined what He has covenanted to do for those who listen to Him, obey His Word, and believe by faith. Ever since the beginning of church history, the devil has worked overtime to remove, discredit, and destroy the Word of God in the earth. The Word is the basis by which we live. It is our sure foundation. God and His Word are one. He cannot destroy God's Word, but what his strategy has been is to destroy man's faith in the Bible. He challenges its authenticity, its validity, and its relevance.

There are many competing voices claiming to have the truth. But there is only one truth. Satan's success is if he can cause us to doubt the veracity of the Bible. If successful, then half the battle is won. Jesus said, *"Man shall not live by bread alone, but by every word that proceeds from the mouth of God."*

> *"Heaven and earth shall pass away, but My Word shall never pass away."*

The Word is God's instruction to His children regarding our history and His plan of redemption for man. It is the Lord's love letter to His kids. The B-I-B-L-E could be an acronym for basic instructions before leaving earth.

> *"My people are destroyed for a lack of knowledge" (Hosea 4:6).*
>
> *Proverbs 29:18 says, "Where there is no vision [no redemptive revelation of God], the people cast off restraint."*

When there is no knowledge of God's Word or His principles in a society, there is social chaos and destruction. In our day, there is a real lack of knowledge of God in most countries around the world. The result is violence, crime, corruption, and evil in the land.

God said, "My people are destroyed for a lack of knowledge." When God's people are ignorant of the Word of God and the principles that are contained in it, then they are going to experience destruction. In addition, if God's people do not have the wisdom to live life according to God's Word, they will go under (Word Wealth, *Spirit-Filled Life Bible for Students* 1995).

Why is the Word of God important to our lives?

Simply, when someone is born again, they are a new creation. As new believers, we have to nourish our spirit man with the Word of God.

> *"As newborn babes, desire the pure milk of the Word, that you may grow thereby." 1 Peter 2:2*

Newborn babies constantly desire milk for nourishment. No sooner do you give them one bottle than they want another and cry loudly until they get it. Their desire for milk is red hot. God wants His people to desire the Word with the same kind of intensity that babies want milk. A sign of spiritual health is an intense desire for the Word.

The Word of God is food for our spirit. Our spirit, nourished by it, transforms our soul; our transformed soul powered by our spirit will subdue our physical body and make it comply with the Word of God. The enemy does everything he can to *separate* us from the Word of God because *faith comes by hearing and by hearing the Word of God.*

Without the proper feeding on His Word, the spirit of a man is negatively affected. When this happens, the dictates of the soul and flesh become predominant in the believer's life. The Word of God helps us subdue our flesh. It changes our thinking in such a way that old mind-sets are deleted and new thoughts, attitudes, ideals are programmed. Nevertheless, if you are content and never allow God's Word to abide in you, you will be subject to the cravings of your flesh and out-of-control soul. The Bible identifies this type of Christian as a carnal Christian. Everything is filtered through the lenses of the flesh. The Word is our connection to the Father. Jesus is identified as the Word incarnate.

> *"In the beginning was the Word and the Word was God and the Word was with God and the Word was God Himself. He was present originally with God. All things were made and came into existence through Him and without Him was not even one thing made that has come into being." John 1:1–3*

We can do nothing apart from the Word and the Holy Spirit. The Word and the Holy Spirit agree. Jesus and the Father agree. Therefore, the Father, Jesus, the Holy Spirit, and the Word all agree. They flow harmoniously together. Jesus was the fulfillment of all the law. Jesus did nothing except what He saw His Father do. He said nothing except what He heard the Father say. Jesus is called the Word of God. The Word was made flesh and dwelt among us. God prophesied concerning the coming Redeemer. If the word spoken by God's prophets and kings can become reality, then we—the Body of Christ—can speak His Word and it can and will become reality in our lives. He was the Word incarnate, Jesus Christ, who defeated Satan. Therefore, it is no surprise his strategy is to diminish the Word in the eyes of the believer. He sows doubt among God's people that the Word may not work, and he whispers, "Of course, it may not work for you." Brother Kenneth Hagin used to say, *"We can't stop the birds from flying over our heads, but we can stop them from making a nest."* In other words, we cannot stop the thoughts that come to us, but we surely can stop those thoughts from taking root in our minds. We are to *cast down every thought and high thing that exalts itself against the knowledge of God.* We are exhorted to only believe! The Word of God is a sure foundation upon which we can absolutely rely upon.

> *"Therefore, whoever hears these sayings of Mine, and does them, I will liken him to a wise man/woman who built his house on the rock: and the rain descended, the floods came and the winds blew and beat on that house; and it did not fall, for it was founded on the rock. But everyone who hears these sayings of Mine and does not do them, will be like a foolish man who built his house on the sand: and the rain descended, the floods came and the winds blew and beat on that house and it fell. And great was its fall."* Matthew 7:24–27

Saints, we should not fall prey to this tactic of the devil. The Word will transform us. It will renew our minds and cause us to think better than we have thought before. The Word will heal your body. The Word will change how you speak. The Word will change everything about you. If the Word of God was not important, then why has so much energy and resources been expended to attack its credibility? The Word of the Lord is forever settled in heaven. Heaven and earth shall pass away, but God's Word shall never pass away. As believers, we ought always to look from an eternal viewpoint.

The Word is the essential element in prayer. The prayers of the saints should be filled with faith and power. When we pray God's Word, there is a guarantee attached to it. God said in Isaiah 55:11, *"So shall My Word* be that goes forth from My mouth; It shall not return to Me void (empty), But it shall accomplish what I please, and it shall prosper in the thing for which I sent it."

Our Father is inviting us to pray His Word back to Him because it will accomplish all He pleases. Praying with confidence and faith will eliminate the beggarly attitude that many have approached the Father with. He said to come boldly to the throne of grace and let your request be made known. This confidence derives from the Word of God. We'll talk more about this in the chapter *If You Ain't Praying*.

If the Bible was no longer relevant to today's society, then why the attacks against the Word? Truth is, it is very much relevant. God's Word never changes. It is timeless. It is relevant for all seasons—past, present, and future. As believers, we cannot afford to live without it. The Word works.

(4) My favorite narrative: that we are born-again believers, but we don't believe anything good will happen for us.

We have become adept at believing the negative reports from sources other than the Lord Himself. Why have we been so willing to accept what the world says about us rather than what God says about us? We are under grace and not under the law. God is not mad at us. Actually, He is in a good mood. He placed all His wrath and judgment on Jesus. Jesus died for our sins and paid the price for our sinful condition. He redeemed mankind through His shed blood and resurrection. From that time forward, the Lord has made His grace available to every believer. His grace is sufficient for us. His grace is powerful. His grace is enough. Jesus is the full expression of the Father's heart. Jesus embodies the character and nature of God.

> *"Have I been with you so long, and yet you have not known Me, Phillip? He who has seen Me has seen the Father; so how can you say, Show us the Father? Do you not believe*

> *that I am in the Father and the Father in Me? The words that I speak to you I do not speak on My own authority; but the Father who dwells in Me does the works." John 14:9–10 Student Life Bible*

We kn*ow that* everything Jesus said and did while He was on the earth was an expression of the will of God. So if we want to know what God desires to do for us today or how He thinks toward us, just look at the ministry of Jesus. Jesus is the mirror image of the Father.

Acts 10:38 says, *"How God anointed Jesus of Nazareth with the Holy Ghost and with power; who went about doing good and healing all that were oppressed of the devil; for God was with Him."*

God is good . He wants you healed. He has you on His mind to show you loving kindness. Surely goodness and mercy shall follow you all the days of your life. It is not calamity, destruction, sickness, or poverty following us, but goodness.

> *"For I know the thoughts that I think toward you, says the Lord, thoughts of peace and not of evil, to give you a future and a hope." Jeremiah 29:11*

God has a plan for each of us, a plan that should give us a great hope for our future. It is our destiny. But that plan is a possibility, not a "positively." If someone prophesies over us wonderful things in the name of the Lord, what they say to us may express the heart, the will, and the desire of God for us. But that does not mean it is positively going to happen just as it is prophesied. This is because it cannot and will not come to pass if we choose to refuse to cooperate with God or if we stray from His will.

God does have a plan for our lives, but we have to participate in that plan for it to come true. God will not force it on you. He is looking for our cooperation. We need to cooperate with God every single day of our lives in order for our potential to be developed. Every day we ought to learn something. Every day we ought to grow. Every day we ought to discover something. Every day we ought to be a bit further along than we were the day before. We should be lifetime learners. God has a plan for each of us. It is a good plan, an uncommon plan, a great plan; it is not an average, mediocre plan. Seek that plan for your life and cooperate with God so that it will be wonderfully fulfilled in your life (*The Everyday Life Bible*).

We have a great inheritance in Jesus just waiting for us to claim it. *Grace and peace be multiplied to you in the knowledge of God and of Jesus our Lord, as His divine power has given to us all things that pertain to life and godliness, through the knowledge of Him who called us by glory and virtue, by which have been given to us exceedingly great and precious promises, that through these you may be partakers of the divine nature.* He has only good stored up for His children. We have been lied to, brethren. We have been told falsehoods about our God. We must rewrite the narrative by which we have been living. If we don't believe anything good will happen to us or for us, then what on earth are we believing? It's a no-brainer that evil exits. The one leading the charge is the devil. There is nothing good about him. He is evil continually.

> *"The thief does not come except to steal, to kill, and to destroy. I came that they may have and enjoy life and have it in abundance to the full, till it overflows." (John 10:10 Amplified Bible)*

You will not know what the Lord has made available to you if you don't get into the Word of God. You see, the treasures of the kingdom will be found when we search them out. Anyone can read the Bible. And many come away not having received anything from it. Realize this, the Bible was not written for the unsaved. Though the unsaved can read it and get saved. The Bible speaks to the Jews and to born-again believers. The Revelator of the Word is the Holy Spirit. He will reveal the hidden secrets to the family of God. As He opens up the Word to us, we discover what great riches have been set aside for us. We'll begin to see ourselves through the eyes of God. We'll discover that we are more than conquerors through Him that loved us. We'll learn about the love of God. And how His love is not an earthly, man-centered love. His love for us is not conditional. It is agape love, an unconditional love. His love is not predicated on what I did or what I haven't done. We cannot deserve God's love. God loved us first, and He pours His love into us so we can love Him, ourselves, and others.

Scripture says, *"That God so loved the world that He gave His only begotten Son. That whosoever believeth on Him will have everlasting life."*

The aforementioned scripture encapsulates the essence of who God is. God so loved His creation, *man-kind*, that He was not willing to allow us to remain in the fallen condition of sin. He had redemption on His mind when He sent His Son to be the propitiation for our sins.

> *"And He Himself is the propitiation for our sins, and not for ours only but also for the whole world." 1 John 2:2*

> *"In this the love of God was manifested toward us, that God has sent His only begotten Son into the world, that we might live through Him. In this is love, not that we loved God, but that He loved us and sent His Son to be the propitiation for our sins." 1 John 4:9–10*

If God were the mean taskmaster waiting for us to make a mistake to strike us down, the kind of God that religion and society has portrayed Him as, then He should have left us in our unregenerate condition because our sentence was eternal separation from Him. But that is not who our God is! He is love. He is Father. He is a giver. He is Holy. He is Savior. He is a Healer. He is a Provider. He is all-powerful. He is Omnipresent. He is all-knowing and much more. Whatever the Lord says, is. The Word of God will debunk erroneous teachings and misconceptions about who we are as God's beloved ones. The only way we can believe correctly is to know the truth. Jesus said, "*If you abide in My Word, you are My disciples indeed. And you shall know the truth, and the truth shall <u>make</u> you free." John 8:31–32*

The key is abiding in His Word. Then you will know the truth, and the truth of the revealed Word will make you free. Most people misquote this scripture. We must first allow the Word to make its home in our lives. And when it does, the Word will begin to push out all that is contrary to God's truth.

The word *make means to liberate; to deliver.* The Word will deliver us from bad theology, other opinions, and lies advocated endeavoring to keep us as captives. Jesus declared that He came to set the captives free. We must turn the switch of faith on and believe the Lord and His holy Word. The Word of God is vital to a believer's growth and development. With it God framed the worlds. With it the worlds are sustained. And with it God reveals Himself to His children. The Word is food for our soul. In order for a believer to believe, to have faith in prayer, and to have a hopeful expectation that something good is going to happen to them, the Word of God must be involved. The Word creates an inner image of the will of God, affording us the opportunity to see ourselves the way God sees us. We are called believers and not doubters. Only believe. *Taste and see that the Lord is good.*

(5) And finally, the granddaddy of them all, a narrative that says all power was given to Jesus, but His church has to limp along powerless, ineffective, inefficient, and fearful of a defeated foe.

What kind of Church is the Lord Jesus building? When He says that He is building His Church and the gates of hell shall not prevail against it, then the Church must have some measure of power, right? Historically, at the beginning of the Church age (read the book of Acts), the Church operated in power, miracles, and lived supernaturally.

> *"But you shall receive power (ability, efficiency and might) when the Holy Spirit has come upon you, and you shall be My witnesses in Jerusalem and all Judea and Samaria and to the ends of the earth." (Acts 1:8 Amplified)*

We need the power Jesus promised. God desires for us to be powerful and live and enjoy power-packed lives. Lives that include victory over Satan and all his wicked plots and schemes.

The Holy Spirit is the enabling power of God, and when He comes into our lives, He enables us to live a supernatural life. We might even say that our power level is dependent on the level that we surrender to Him. Have you surrendered every room in your heart to the Holy Spirit? Have you invited Him into every area of your life, or do you reserve certain areas for yourself where you want no interference from anyone, not even God? Is there a Do Not Disturb sign on the door of your heart? If so, invite Him in. We cannot be who He has called us to be without transformation. He is the Potter and we are the clay. Stay on the wheel and allow the Master to fashion you into the likeness of Jesus. It will require a dying to self and taking up the cross of Jesus. If you truly want to live for God, this is the process we all must go through. There are no shortcuts. I suppose Jesus may have thought there must be a different way than going to the cross. We see in the Garden of Gethsemane His struggle with His flesh and the Father's will.

> *"Then they went a place called Gethsemane, and He said to His disciples, Sit down here while I pray. And He took with Him Peter and James and John and began to be struck with terror and amazement and deeply troubled and depressed. And He said to them, My soul is exceedingly sad (overwhelmed with grief) so that it almost kills Me! Remain here and keep awake and be watching. And going a little farther, He fell on the ground and kept praying that if it were possible for the [fatal] hour might pass from Him. And He was saying, Abba, Father, everything is possible for*

> *You. Take away this cup from Me; yet not what I will, but what You will." Mark 14: 32–36 Amplified*

Twice Jesus came back and found the disciples sleeping. He charged them to keep awake and pray. He went away again and prayed the same words. Certainly Jesus was struggling with having to go to the cross. But in the end, He submitted to the will of the Father. Like Jesus, we'll have to make a decision about which path to go down. Will it be the self-directed path or the God-directed path? When we choose God's way, it always leads to life.

Spiritual maturity is a process. We release areas of our lives to the Lord, little by little. The more we release to Him, the better our lives become. The power of the Holy Spirit enables us to be what God wants us to be. God wants us to *be* witnesses rather than witnessing. God is more interested in our *becoming* than in our doing. God wants us to become what He has in mind for us, and then out of that we will begin to do what He wants us to do. God's deepest desire for each of us is that we become like Christ in our thoughts, attitudes, words, and deeds.

The Body of Christ is not void of power. Jesus delegated power to His disciples before He went to the cross.

> *"Behold, I give you the authority to trample on serpents and scorpions and over all the power of the enemy, and nothing shall by any means hurt you." Luke 10:19*

The enemy of the Church wants us to think we are powerless. Jesus is our supreme example. When He walked the earth, the demons yelled and pleaded with Him when He approached someone who was demon possessed. Jesus walked in authority and power given to Him by the Father. He demonstrated authority over the elements, over sickness and disease, over creation and over death. He defied the physical laws and was Lord over them. Satan heard God say, *"This is My beloved Son, in whom I am well pleased."* He knew exactly who Jesus was. Satan used the religious leaders who plotted to kill Jesus. And when they tried, Jesus just walked right through the crowd. But they finally succeeded when it was time for Him to be the sacrificial Lamb.

We have been authorized by the Lord Jesus to advance the kingdom of God everywhere we go. Jesus said He was building His Church and the gates of hell shall not prevail against it. Gates are stationary. It's the Church that is on the move. I have not seen a gate run after anyone, trying to prevent them from going anywhere.

When you made Jesus Christ the Lord of your life, you were delivered from the power of darkness. The word power is translated authority. You have been delivered from the power or authority of darkness and placed in God's kingdom. Jesus succeeded in securing all power by going to the cross, dying a horrible death, suffering the penalty of sin, and defeating Satan in the pit of hell. After securing the authority and power, He freely delegated it to those who would believe in Him.

> Jesus commanded *"to go into all the world and preach and publish openly the good news to every creature of the whole human race. He who believes and is baptized will be saved; but he who does not believe in Him will be condemned. And these attesting signs will accompany those who believe; in My name they will drive out demons; they will speak in new languages; they will pick up serpents and even if the drink anything deadly, it will not hurt them; they will lay their hands on the sick and they will get well."* Mark 16:15–18 The Everyday Life Bible

We have an awesome responsibility as messengers of the covenant of grace. The Father knew we could not accomplish this task in our own strength. In our strength, we are no match for the devil. But thanks to God that we don't have to operate in our strength. God has given us another comforter, the same comforter who was with Jesus during His earthly ministry, the Holy Spirit.

> *"How God anointed Jesus of Nazareth with the Holy Spirit and with strength and ability and power; how He went about doing good and in particular, curing all who were harassed and oppressed by the devil, for God was with Him." Acts 10:38*

The church by and large must recognize that we are loaded. We are loaded with God's grace, God's anointing, God's power, God's Word, God's Spirit, angelic host, Jesus' blood, the finished work of the cross, and so much more.

We are not powerless, but powerful. We are not ineffective, but effectual. We are not inefficient, but judicious and methodical. We are not fearful of a defeated foe, but bold as lions.

We have the power of God's Word and the backing of heaven to execute God's purpose in the earth.

> *"And the same day, when the evening was come, He said unto them, Let us pass over unto the other side. And when they had sent away the multitude, they took Him even as he was in the ship. And there were also with Him other little ships. And there arose a great storm of wind, and the waves beat into the ship, so that it was now full. And He was in the hinder part of the ship, asleep on a pillow: and they awake Him, and say unto Him, Master, don't you care that we perish? And He arose, and rebuked the wind, and said unto the sea, Peace, be still. And the wind ceased, and there was a great calm. And He said unto them, why are you so fearful? How is it that you have no faith?" Mark 4:35–40*

Jesus spoke the words, "Let us pass over unto the other side." There was enough power and authority in those words to accomplish the job. One thing I want you to notice is that Jesus did not take command of the ship to ensure His words were carried out. He walked to the back of the boat and went to sleep. Jesus delegated the authority to His disciples, and they accepted it. But when the storm arose, they were filled with fear of the boat sinking. Jesus carried out the responsibility of authority, which He had delegated to them, by rebuking the wind and the sea.

Do you see the parallel here? You are the captain of your ship. You have control over your own life—your spirit, your soul, and your body. As captains our job is to depend on the navigator, the Holy Spirit to guide and lead us in the ways we should go.

> *"Behold, I give you the authority to trample on serpents and scorpions and over all the power (ability) of the enemy, AND nothing shall by any means hurt you." Luke 10:19*

You are to give the devil no place in your life. You are born of the Spirit of God. You are filled with the Spirit of God. You have been given the Word of God. Those three elements are enough for us to fulfill our spiritual assignment on earth. You don't need any more power. You have all the power necessary. You simply have to exercise your authority. Jesus has already done everything necessary to secure the authority and power over sin, sickness, demons, and fear. You have to employ faith to receive that authority and join forces with Him in this earth. You are called to be strong in the Lord and in the power of His might.

Now is the time for us to discard the false narratives that have held believers in bondage.

Jesus said, *"If you abide in My word, you are My disciples indeed. And you shall know the truth, and the truth shall make you free."* John 8: 31–32

The prerequisite to knowing the truth is first having the Word of God abiding in your heart. The Word should be settled and permanent in our hearts. The Word is a discerner of good and bad, right and wrong, godly and ungodly. We need the Word just like we need air to breathe. Without God's Word, we can and will be susceptible to plausible arguments and narratives. We cannot afford to live our lives any longer as though we are a people without hope in this world. We are loaded. We are loaded, and some folks don't even know it.

If you have believed the lies of the aforementioned narratives, then repent to the Lord and ask Him to lead you down His paths of righteousness. Ask the Father to reveal erroneous doctrines in your life. Ask the Father to reveal areas of unbelief in your life. Then surrender your life to the working of the Holy Spirit. God is waiting for His children to make His kingdom principles a reality. He is waiting for His people to be in hot pursuit of righteousness. He is waiting for us to receive and enter into all of the spiritual experiences available in the restored Church. We are to prove all things and hold fast to that which is good. We will press on toward the mark for the prize of that high calling of God in Christ Jesus.

A wholesome tongue is a tree of life.
(Proverbs 15:4)

CHAPTER 2

SAY IT AIN'T SO

I cannot begin to tell you how many times in my Christian experience I've heard believers discount the spiritual principle of our words having creative power. They are so eager to challenge the validity of that truth that they clearly miss the evidence before them. Man is the only creation authorized by God to choose his words and to use those words in a constructive or destructive manner. Early in my walk with the Lord, I came across a man named Charles Capps. Brother Capps has taught extensively concerning words and their creative power. We were formed in the likeness of God. God spoke everything into existence.

> *"In the beginning was the Word, and the Word was with God and the Word was God. All things were made by Him; and without Him was not anything made that was made." John 1:1, 3*

All things were made by Him. Without Him was not anything made that was made. Jesus is called the Word. He is the Word personified.

> *"For it was in Him that all things were created, in heaven and on earth, things seen and things unseen, whether thrones, dominions, rulers, or authorities; all things were created and exist through Him and in and for Him.*
>
> *And He Himself existed before all things, and in Him all things consist (cohere, are held together)." Colossians 1:16–17 (The Everyday Life Bible)*

Everything was created by Him, and by the Word all things consist. *"Through faith we understand that the worlds were framed by the word of God, so that things which are seen were not made of things which do appear." Hebrews 11:3*

It was through faith that the worlds were formed. The earth, the stars, the solar system, and every living thing created by God who first spoke them into existence. It was not a big bang and poof here we are nor was it by evolution. By the way, Darwin, at the end of his life, recanted his theory of evolution. The God of the Bible, the only real God, is completely different from all man-made gods and idols. God is not a ball of energy or a cosmic force. God is a Spirit. He is a personal God and loves us as members of His family. All that we see was created through the spoken Word. In the beginning does not mean in God's beginning. Scripture is very clear that God is eternal. He has no beginning or end. In the beginning is referring to man's beginning. We are finite beings. We have a beginning and an ending. In the book of Genesis, we can clearly see a distinct pattern of creation. God's pattern for creation is to first speak it, and then it manifests.

> *"And **God said**, Let there be light; and there was light. And God saw that the light was good and He approved it; and God separated the light from the darkness. And God called the light Day, and the darkness He called Night. And there was evening and there was morning, one day. And **God said**, let there be a firmament [the expanse of the sky] in the midst of the waters, and let it separate the waters [below] from the waters [above]. And God made the firmament [the expanse] and separated the waters which were under the expanse from the waters which were above the expanse. And it was so. And God called the firmament Heavens. And there was evening and there was morning, a second day. And **God said**, Let the waters under the heavens be collected into one place, and let the dry land appear. And it was so. God called the dry land Earth, and the accumulated waters He called Seas. And God saw that this was good and He approved it. And **God said**, Let the earth put forth vegetation: plants yielding seed and fruit trees yielding fruit whose seed is in itself, each according to its kind upon the earth. And it was so. And there was evening and there was morning, a third day. And **God said**, Let there be lights in the expanse of the heavens to separate the day from the night, and let them be signs and*

tokens of God's provident care and to mark the seasons, days, and years. And let them be lights in the expanse of the sky to give light upon the earth. And it was so. And God made the two great lights, the greater light (the sun) to rule the day and the lesser light (the moon) to rule the night. He also made the stars. And God set them in the expanse of the heavens to give light upon the earth. And God saw that it was good and He approved it. And there was evening and there was morning, a fourth day. And __God said__, let the waters bring forth abundantly and swarm with living creatures, and let birds fly over the earth in the open expanse of the heavens. God created the great sea monsters and every living creature that moves, which the waters brought forth abundantly, according to their kinds and every winged bird according to its kind. And God saw that it was good and He approved it. And God blessed them, __saying__, Be fruitful, multiply and fill the waters in the seas, and let the fowl multiply in the earth. And there was evening and there was morning, a fifth day. And __God said,__ Let the earth bring forth living creatures according to their kinds; livestock, creeping things and wild beast of the earth according to their kinds. And it was so. And God saw that it was good and He approved it. And __God said,__ Let US [Father, Son and Holy Spirit] make mankind in Our image, after Our likeness, and let them have complete authority over the fish of the sea, the birds of the air, the beast and over all the earth, and over everything that creeps upon the earth. So God created man in His own image, in the image and likeness of God He created him; male and female He created them. And __God blessed them and said to them.__ Be fruitful, multiply and replenish the earth and subdue it [using its vast resources in the service of God and man]; and have dominion over the fish of the sea, the birds of the air, and over every living creature that moves upon the earth." Genesis 1:3–28

Preceding the creation of a thing, God speaks. Once God said "let there be," the Son then commissioned the Holy Spirit to execute the orders, and the Holy Spirit carried out the orders.

The Genesis account of creation demonstrates how words were the vehicle God used in the spiritual realm to make things happen in the physical or natural realm. When God, who is spirit, wanted something material created, He spoke first. We have been given the authority and commission to act just like Daddy God. The Bible is replete with scriptures illustrating this truth. What we have failed to recognize is, once the Lord completed His work of creation, He then turned over the maintaining of the earth to Adam. God's instruction to Adam was to be <u>fruitful</u>, <u>multiply</u>, <u>replenish the earth</u>, <u>subdue it</u>, and <u>have dominion over every living creature.</u>

The meaning of the underlined words are as follows:

Fruitful—*means to grow, increase.*

Multiply—*means to increase (in whatever respect), bring in abundance, enlarge, excel, exceedingly, be full of, and be great.*

Replenish—*means to refill.*

Subdue—*to tread down, to conquer, keep under, bring into subjection.*

Dominion—*to tread down, subjugate, prevail against, reign, rule over.*

Now let us reread this verse with the definitions attached to it.

> "So God created man in His own image; in the image of God He created him; male and female He created them. Then God blessed them, and God said to them, "Be fruitful, grow and increase and multiply in whatever respect, bring in abundance and enlarge yourselves, excel exceedingly and be full and be great in all you do; replenish, fill up

again, build up again the earth and subdue it, bring it into subjection to your ruler-ship and finally have dominion, reign and rule and prevail over every living thing that moves on the earth."

Whew! I don't know about you, but that makes me want to dance and shout, Hallelujah! God has not rescinded those orders. We have fallen short of what the Lord commanded us to do in the garden. The result of Adam's sin changed the line of authority. It no longer was God the Father, God the Son, God the Holy Spirit, man and creation, which included angels and demons. The Fall put the devil in the position where man should have been. Consequently, God the Son had to be born of a woman, making Him a legitimate authority to legislate and adjudicate on behalf of all mankind. Once divine justice was satisfied by Jesus dying on the cross and going to hell for three days and nights, He then arose from the grave to be the Executor of the New Testament signed in His blood. Man was returned back to his place of authority in the earth. The devil was rendered powerless. His weapons now are fear, lies, and deception, of which he is a master craftsman.

So, what is the significance?

The enemy cannot speak and command anything to happen in the earth. He needs earthlings to parrot his lies, his deceptions, and his fears. That's why he whispers into our ears all sorts of ungodly things, hoping that we would speak them. When we spend time meditating on the lies of the enemy, they will eventually affect our emotions, which influence our decision making. If we're making wrong decisions based on incorrect information, then we receive the wrong results. The Bible is clear concerning capturing every thought and subjecting them to the Word of God. The Word is a filter. It will differentiate what is good and bad. Do not allow the enemy to rent space in your mind. You've got to say something. Say it ain't so! When he comes to you, peddling his lies, you must say it ain't so. However, if you don't know it's a lie, then how can you say it ain't so if you don't know it ain't so? This is where some lose their footing. They won't take the time to study the Word for themselves. They are content with attending church on Sundays, hoping the snack they receive will be sustainable for the entire week. We are supposed to read, pray, and believe God for ourselves. We are supposed to fellowship with the Lord daily. We are exhorted to desire the milk of the Word so that we may grow thereby. God wants His people to desire the Word of God with the same kind of intensity that babies want milk. A sign of spiritual health is an intense desire for the Word.

> *"For the Word of God is living and powerful, and sharper than any two edged sword, piercing even to the division of soul and spirit and of joints and marrow and is a discerner of the thoughts and intents of the heart." Hebrews 4:12*

Every Word from the Bible is filled with the same power that resurrected Christ from the dead and that which created the universe. The Word of God is a living and powerful Word, which is able to penetrate the very depths of our subconscious being. The Word of God has the power to go beyond our conscious mind to the very core of our spiritual being to cleanse, convict, and transform us. The Word can tear down strongholds of fear, failure, lust, and negativity and then build powerful new habit patterns that produce life, love, and liberty. God's ultimate plan for our lives is for Christ to be formed in us.

Restoration of our souls begin when we partner with the Word and declare what He says about us. When you are bombarded with thoughts of defeat, go to the Word and search out scriptures identifying you as victorious, as more than conquerors and as over-comers. Let the redeemed of the Lord say so. Our hearts should be full of the Word. *Whatever is in your heart in abundance the mouth will eventually speak. That is a spiritual law.* What about when sickness comes knocking at your door? Do you open the door and say *"Come on in, I've been expecting you,"* or do you go to God's Word on the subject and declare what God says?

"**Surely, absolutely** He has borne our griefs and carried our sorrows; yet we esteemed Him stricken, smitten by God, and afflicted. But He was wounded for our transgressions, He was bruised for our iniquities; the chastisement for our peace was upon Him, And by His stripes we are healed." Isaiah 53:4–5

"My God is the Lord who heals me." Exodus 15:26

"No evil will befall me. Neither shall any plaque come near my dwelling place." Psalm 91:10

"The Lord heals all my diseases." Psalm 103:3

"He sent His Word and healed me and delivered me from my destruction." Psalm 107:20

"God's Word is health and medicine to all my flesh." Proverbs 4:22

"Jesus went about doing good and healing all who were oppressed of the devil." Acts 10:38

"Christ has redeemed me from the curse of the law, being made a curse for me. The blessing of Abraham has come upon me through Jesus Christ." Galatians 3:13–14

"The prayer of faith saves the sick and the Lord raises him up." James 5:15

"Beloved, I pray above all else that you may prosper and be in health just as your soul prospers." 3 John 2

Our jobs have been made simple because our Father has provided what we need, His word. The Word of God is both a defensive and offensive weapon. No wonder the battle intensifies when a believer is word dependent.

Warfare is our way of life

We are told to wage a good warfare. Take the sword of the Spirit, which is the Word of God, and use it skillfully against the demonic realm. We are not the sick trying to get healed. We are the healed who are contending against opposing forces attempting to steal our health. Beloved, the price for our healing was paid for. The price for our salvation has been paid for. The price for our deliverance has been paid for. Whatever was not right with humanity was corrected through Jesus Christ. Everything that was lost in the garden because of Adam's disobedience, Jesus restored back to man and much more. Brethren, we are never fighting from a position of defeat but rather from a position of victory. Jesus has won the war. We must now enforce His victory on a rebellious, rogue, prideful fallen spirit name Satan.

Our warfare should never be with people. We contend with evil spirits that oppress and possess people. Jesus confronted a man who had an unclean spirit. The unclean spirit caused him to commit self-destructive acts, which might have eventually led to suicide. Jesus went to the root of the problem.

> *"Then they came to the other side of the sea, to the country of the Gadarenes. And when they had come out of the boat, immediately there met Him out of the tombs a man with an unclean spirit, who had his dwelling among the tombs; and no one could bind him, not even with chains, because he had often been bound with shackles and chains. And the chains had been pulled apart by him, and the shackles broken in pieces; neither could anyone tame him. And always, night and day, he was in the mountains and in the*

> *tombs, crying out and cutting himself with stones. When he saw Jesus from afar, he ran and worshiped Him. And he cried out with a loud voice and said, 'What have I to do with You, Jesus, Son of the Most High God? I implore You by God that You do not torment me.'*
>
> *For He said to him, 'Come out of the man, unclean spirit!' Then He asked him, 'What is your name?' And he answered saying, 'My name is Legion; for we are many.' Also he begged Him earnestly that He would not send them out of the country. Now a large herd of swine was feeding there near the mountains. So all the demons begged Him, saying, 'Send us to the swine, that we may enter them.' And at once Jesus gave them permission. Then the unclean spirits went out and entered the swine (there about two thousand); and the herd ran violently down the steep place into the sea, and drowned in the sea.*
>
> *Then they came to Jesus, and saw the one who had been demon-possessed and had the legion, sitting and clothed and in his **right mind**. And they were afraid."*
> Mark 5:1–13, 15

Jesus commanded these unclean spirits to leave and gave them permission to enter an entire herd of pigs, which ran into the sea and drowned. The man was set free and restored to his right mind. Many people in society are contending with demonic forces. There is an increase of self-destructive behavior. There are many who are diagnosed with psychological problems and acts of violence have spiked.

We have a culture that is spinning out of control. More and more movies are depicting demonic activity. I believe it is Hollywood's attempt to mainstream or normalize demonic activity. Our culture has demonstrated a penchant for the occult and dark side of the spirit world. While in many quarters, the church sits wondering what in the world is going on. We shake our heads saying things like, "I just don't know what this world is coming to." Or we blame our politicians for the condition of our society. Or we shift blame to other things rather than look ourselves squarely in the mirror. Jesus said that we are the salt of the world. We are the light of the world. Salt is a preserver. We are supposed to preserve the society in which we live. What good is salt in the salt shaker? None! It is meant to be used. As children of the light, why are we content to shine amongst ourselves? It's the world who needs the light. We must come out of the four walls of the church and be the difference maker in our society. We have allowed the world, led by ungodly men and women, to dictate to the Body of Christ our role in society.

> *"For we do not wrestle with flesh and blood, but against principalities, against powers, against the rulers of the darkness of this age, against spiritual host of wickedness in the heavenly places." Ephesians 6:12*

We are commanded to be strong in the Lord and in the power of His might. We don't engage the enemy in our strength but in the strength of God. We must be armed with the Word of God and clothed in the love of God. We get our marching orders from the Spirit of God. We must clean up our act and stop being a double-minded people. We have a responsibility before God to do the works of Jesus like He commanded. This responsibility is not just for pastors and leaders either. We all have been delegated to change the atmosphere in our homes, our cities, our nation, and the world. We are to subdue, subjugate and have dominion over demonic forces and not the other way around. Our mandate is the following:

> *"Behold, I have given you all authority to trample on serpents and scorpions and over all the power of the enemy and nothing shall in any way harm you." Luke 10:19*

> *"Go into all the world and preach the gospel (good news) to every creation. He who believes and is baptized will be saved; but he who does not believe will be condemned. And these signs will follow those who believe: In My name they will cast out demons; they will speak with new tongues; they will take up serpents; and if they drink anything deadly, it will by no means hurt them; they will lay hands on the sick, and they will recover." Mark 16:15–18*

Beloved, we cannot shirk from our responsibility to fight. Our fight is not like a boxer preparing for his next bout, shadow boxing. We were born in a fight. Our weapons, however, are not carnal or man-made things. They are mighty through God to the pulling down of strongholds in our thought life and in the spirit. To be effective against evil forces, the tongue of the believer must come under the control of the Holy Spirit. Allow Him to retrain your speech. Allow the Word to instruct you in righteousness. The Word of God is a highly effective weapon. That is why it is paramount to have right thinking and to know how to skillfully use the Word of God. The words we speak carry great authority. With great authority there is great responsibility.

> *Death and life are in the power of the tongue and those who love it will eat its fruit. Proverbs 18:21*

Jesus demonstrated this when He was in the wilderness fasting. The devil came to Him with a tempting offer.

> *Then Jesus was led up by the Spirit into the wilderness to be tempted by the devil. And when He had fasted forty days and forty nights, afterward He was hungry. Now when the tempter came to Him, he said "If You are the Son of God, command that these stones become bread." But He answered and said,* **"IT IS WRITTEN***, man shall not live by bread alone, but by every word that proceeds from the mouth of God." Then the devil took Him up into the*

holy city, set Him on the pinnacle if the temple, and said to Him, "If You are the Son of God, throw Yourself down. For it is written: "He shall give His angels charge over you, and in their hands they shall bear you up, Lest you dash your foot against a stone."

*Jesus said to him, "**IT IS WRITTEN, AGAIN**, You shall not tempt the Lord your God. And again the devil took Him up on an exceeding high mountain and showed Him all the kingdoms of the world and their glory. And he said to Him, "All these things I will give You if You will fall down and worship me." Then Jesus said to him, "Away with you, Satan! **FOR IT IS WRITTEN**, you shall worship the Lord God and Him only you shall serve." Then the devil left Him and behold, angels came and ministered to Him.*

Did you notice the devil knew the Word of God and how he tried to misapply it? Jesus is the Word made flesh. So, he was trying to deceive the Author and Finisher of the Word. He even challenged Jesus' identity. He heard God say, "This is My Beloved Son, in whom I am well pleased." And yet he questioned, "If You are the Son of God." Beloved, he will do the same to us. We must become students of the Word so that when the enemy approaches us, we will be able to stand in our day of temptation. However, we must be intimately acquainted with the Father's Word. Knowing *about* the Word will not suffice. His Word must be abiding in us to such a degree that it speaks to us. God works through His written Word. He established everything through His Word. A significant part of the devil's plan is to separate God's people from God's Word. Without knowing His Word, you and I cannot know the will of God. God and His Word are one. The Word is a lamp unto our feet. The Word purifies us, it corrects us, it guides us, it reveals the hidden mysteries of the kingdom to us and it reveals who we are in Christ. It is health and life to us, and much, much more. Without the Word, we cannot have faith. Without faith it is impossible to please

God. Inherent in the Word is faith. That is why we are exhorted to continue hearing the Word.

> *"So, then faith cometh by hearing and hearing by the Word of God." Romans 10:17*

The Word of God illuminated by the Holy Spirit is the only true means for transforming the human heart. Spiritual disciples devour God's Word because it is the key to a more dynamic relationship with their living Lord. God told Joshua to keep the commandments and do according to all the law that Moses commanded them.

> *"The Book of the Law shall not depart from your mouth, but you shall meditate in it day and night, that you may observe to do according to all that is written in it.* ***For then**** you will make your way prosperous, and then you will have good success." Joshua 1:8*

We cannot successfully wage a good warfare without the Word. His Word is the sword of the spirit. It is one of the most effective weapons we have. Every place and everything the Church have relinquished, we are commanded to reclaim them. Take back ground we have given up to Satan. We must again be a voice in this nation and not an echo. We are the glorious, overcoming church. And it is time we begin acting like it! There is much to be done before our Lord's return. It is time for lambs to become lions.

The tongue, a little member

We are more circumspect over what we put into our mouths instead of what is coming out of it. Personally, I cannot eat just anything. I have a sensitive stomach; therefore, I am guarded over what I eat. I remember a time in college, I attended a house party, and there was food galore. I asked someone about a particular dish and what were the ingredients. Well, no one in the immediate area could tell me what the dish was, so against my better judgment, I decided to give it a try. I spent the next two days sick as I could be. From that time forward, I have made it a point not to eat anything questionable or from anyone with questionable hygiene habits. In Jesus' day, the religious leaders did much of what they did for outward show. They wanted to be seen by men and for the people to think of them as spiritual. They had all the appearances of being righteous men, but on the inside, they were as dead men. Along comes Jesus and this is what He says,

> *"These people draw near to Me with their mouth, and honor Me with their lips, but their heart is far from Me. And in vain they worship Me, teaching as doctrines the commandments of men." When He had called the multitude to Himself, He said to them, "Hear, and understand: Not what goes into the mouth defiles a man, but what comes out of the mouth, this defiles a man." Then His disciples came and said to Him, "Do you know that the Pharisees were offended when they heard this saying?" But He answered and said, "Every plant which My Heavenly Father has not planted will be uprooted. Let them alone. They are blind leaders of the blind. And if the blind leads the blind, both will fall into a ditch." Then Peter answered and said to Him, "Explain this parable to us." So Jesus said, "Are you also still without understanding? Do you not yet understand that whatever enters the mouth goes into the stomach and is eliminated? But those things which proceed out of the mouth come from the heart, and they defile a man. For out of the heart proceed evil thoughts, murders, adulteries, fornications, thefts, false witness, blasphemies. These are the things which defile a man, but to eat with unwashed hands does not defile a man."*
> Matthew 15:8–20 (Spirit-Filled Life Bible for Students)

Jesus said that they were doing a lot of talking and showboating, but in reality, something totally different was in their heart. The spiritual principle enunciated here is whatever is in your heart in abundance, you will say. So, they were giving Jesus lip service. In their worship of Him, they worshipped Him in vain because they chose the doctrines of men over the doctrines of God. The Pharisees were so accustomed to playacting when Jesus showed up, they did not recognize Him. They continued on with business as usual. Jesus wanted them to know there was a new measuring stick. That measuring stick was whatever words proceeds out of a man's mouth causes the defilements. It is not what goes into one's mouth that defiles but what proceeds out of one's mouth, which comes from the heart, that defiles a man. The Bible has much to say concerning the words we speak. We have been granted an awesome responsibility to speak like God speaks. With this responsibility, we must educate ourselves regarding this little member called the tongue.

Jesus said what He heard the Father say. He did what He saw the Father do. He did not think it robbery to be like God. Think of yourselves the way Christ Jesus thought of Himself. He had equal status with God, but He always showed us the Father. He did not come to bring glory to Himself. He glorified the Father. When He accomplished His assignment, the Father glorified Jesus.

The Father created man as *another speaking spirit*. We were created to speak the oracles of God in the earth. God's divine order was contaminated with sin. Instead of man ruling and reigning over the earth, he was made subject to a fallen spirit, the devil. The devil began sowing weed seeds in the minds of men. And men spoke those very weed seeds contaminating his life and the lives of his family. We must begin to say it ain't so no more! Say what God says about you! Our entire manner of speech must be changed.

We live in a day where speaking negatively is acceptable and, in some cases, encouraged. In just a couple of generations, our culture has thrown off all restraint and eliminated all boundaries where obscenity is concerned. The apostle Paul warned Christian people in his day against the problem of indulging in filthy language. When you live in a culture that bombards you with filthy speech night and day, if we are not careful, we may find ourselves indulging in it. I remember a time when men did not curse around women and children. But those days are long gone. Today women are speaking just as profanely as the men are. And the effects are evident in our children. Our children are emulating what they hear and see at home, in music, and through the various channels of entertainment. We must get a grip on the truth of God's Word. *"By your words you are condemned and by your words you are justified."* You choose which it shall be. The book of James is clear in its explanation of the tongue.

> *"Indeed, we put bits in horse's mouths that they may obey us and we turn their whole body. Look also at ships: although they are so large are driven by fierce winds, they are turned by a very small rudder wherever the pilot desires. Even so the tongue is a little member and boasts great things. See how great a forest a little fire kindles! And the tongue is a fire, a world of iniquity. The tongue is so set among our members that it defiles the whole body, and sets on fire the course of nature and it is set on fire by hell." James 3:3–6*

The tongue a little member among many members, yet it yields the power to set on fire the course of nature. Think of all the problems you could have avoided in life by just shutting your mouth. God has placed awesome power in the tongue. Demon-possessed men have seduced nations with their tongues, while great evangelists have led millions to Christ using theirs. The tongue is a fire, a world of iniquity. What does that mean? The *Amplified Bible* translates, *"And the tongue is a fire. A world of wickedness set among our members contaminating and depraving the whole body and setting on fire the wheel of birth (the cycle of man's nature), being itself ignited by hell."*

The apostle James said that if any man can control his tongue, he is a fully developed character and can control his entire being. No man can tame the tongue. We need God's help. King David prayed that God would put a watch over his mouth. David knew he could not control his mouth without God's help and neither can we.

Jesus said take His yoke upon us and learn of Him because He is gentle, meek and humble. A gentle tongue, with its healing power, is a tree of life, but willful contrariness in it breaks down the spirit. We can speak words of healing or words that wound; we can edify and build up or discourage and tear down. Death and life are in the power of the tongue. We make the choice by our words. We can bless ourselves or curse ourselves by the way we speak.

If you have been speaking curses over your life, repent and ask God to render a crop failure of every curse word that you have spoken. Then ask God to put a watch over your mouth so that you would not sin against Him. Remember, Satan is after your words. If he can convince us to say things in opposition to God's Word, then we come out on the losing end. We must stop partnering with the enemy in our words. Allow the Holy Spirit to retrain you. Allow Him to teach you how to speak as a new creation in Christ Jesus. Will it be a challenge? Of course it will, especially if you've allowed your mouth to say everything and anything that comes to your mind. But as you surrender to the leading of the Holy Spirit, He will diligently teach you how to consistently speak words of life. The conforming of our speech happens as a result of renewing the mind.

> *"Do not be conformed to this world (this age), fashioned after and adapted to its external, superficial customs, but be transformed, changed by the entire renewal of your mind by its new ideals and its new attitude, so that you may prove for yourselves what is the good and acceptable and perfect will of God." Romans 12:2*

When the mind is renewed, it will affect a change in our speech. We renew our minds and get new attitudes and new ideals by studying God's Word. His Word is truth. The Word transforms. The Word builds. The Word deletes. Get the picture. The Word works. It is designed by God for us.

> *"Set a guard, O Lord, before my mouth; keep watch at the door of my lips." Psalm 141:3*

As believers, we must ever be mindful that we are instruments of righteousness. Every part of our body belongs to the Lord. If we don't bridle our tongues, we'll never accomplish the purposes of God in our lives. Turn your tongue into a fountain of life rather than a fire hose of destruction. No man can tame the tongue. But the Holy Spirit can! Simply allow the Lord to speak to you through the scriptures. Stop being the devil's mouthpiece. Stop speaking death over your health, your finances, your marriage, and your relationships. Start allowing your mouth to line up with the Word of God. Your words either build up or tear down. It's one or the other because words, more than anything else, connect us to God and to each other.

"We do not have the right to speak 'freely' at all times; we cannot claim that we were 'just kidding' when we break hearts and spirits with our words; and we are deceived if we believe that our negative words evaporate into thin air and are quickly forgotten. But positive words can bring healing, and they have no expiration date" (Morris, *The Power of Your Words*).

Since we are free moral agents, the Lord will not make us say the right words. He has given us His Word and instructed us to say His Word. His warning to us is this,

> *"Death and life are in the power of the tongue." Proverbs 18:21*

> *"I call heaven and earth to witness this day against you that I have set before you life and death, the blessings and the curses; therefore, choose life that you and your descendants may live." Deuteronomy 30:19*

Notice that what we choose—life or death, blessings or curses—will not only affect our lives but our children and grandchildren also. Take an inventory of what you have been speaking. Examine what doors you opened or what doors you have closed.

The choice is ours to make. What say you?

My house shall be a house of prayer.

CHAPTER 3

IF YOU AIN'T PRAYING

When I was a little girl, I would pray at night for my mother's health and safety. I prayed like most children do—with much fear and trembling, hoping that God would not be annoyed with me for praying the same thing all the time. My perception of God was that He was busy all the time. I would approach the Lord with fear that He may just ignore my little request. Nevertheless, I prayed anyway because that's all I knew to do. My mother was a single parent. She suffered from asthma just about every day. I was afraid that her illness might take her away from us. After becoming an adult, I still had fear anytime I wanted to pray. It wasn't until I was born again and began reading God's Word that I discovered how eager the Father desires for His children to come to Him with our request. It was in this discovery period that I learned how much God loves us. That He is not angry with us, and He is never too busy for us either. In fact, Jesus said *when* you pray. He did not say *if* you pray. Boy, that was a huge breakthrough for me. The truth is, our Father loves us, and He is merciful toward us. He loves it when His children trust Him with every facet of their lives. He loves it when we are wholly dependent on Him.

> "*Now it came to pass, as He was praying in a certain place, when He ceased, that one of His disciples said to Him, 'Lord, teach us to pray, as John also taught his disciples.' So He said to them, 'When you pray say . . .'" Luke 11:1–2*

Jesus gave His disciples a model and a guide for effective praying. Not only did Jesus say, "When you pray, say," but in teaching this prayer, He also said, "In this manner, therefore, pray."

> "*Our Father in heaven, hallowed be Your name. Your kingdom come. Your will be done. On earth as it is in heaven. Give us this day our daily bread. And forgive us our debts, as we forgive our debtors. And do not lead us into temptation, But deliver us from the evil one. For Yours is the kingdom and the power and the glory forever. Amen.*" Matthew 6:9–13

Jesus gave this prayer as a model for us. This prayer model consists of worship, praise, petition, confession of sins, forgiving others, and a prayer for overcoming temptation and the power of the devil. These are prayer dynamics that should be incorporated into prayer. When we pray, we honor God for who He is. We acknowledge His Lordship in our lives. There is nothing in the Word that remotely implies we should cease from praying. In fact, the Bible is clear that we should keep asking, keep seeking, keep believing, and keep knocking. The only one opposed to persistent prayer is the devil. He doesn't want us praying and seeking God about anything. He utilizes his weapons to discourage the believer from praying.

In the kingdom of God, prayer is the vehicle used to transport things from the spirit realm into the physical realm. It is the vehicle of communication between earth and heaven. Simply, prayer is our open line of communication with our Heavenly Father. A strategy in war is to cut the enemies' lines of communication. If communication between headquarters and the frontline troops are disrupted or severed, continuity is lost. The troops will not have orders from their commanders, thereby affecting any tactical positions and forward advancements. On the other end, headquarters would be operating in the blind without status reports from the front line. Prayer for the believer is our lifeline, just as blood is to the human body. Without blood, there is no life. Without an active prayer life, we will not receive the needed directions from our Commander-in-Chief. That's why the enemy fights relentlessly against it.

Think about where our nation would be if prayer had not been taken out of our schools. Mind you, the prayer was a generic one. It called upon God to watch over our nation.

> *"Almighty God, we acknowledge our dependence on thee, and beg thy blessing on us, our teachers, our parents, and our nation. Amen."*

So what is offensive about that? The simplicity of that prayer asked for the Lord's blessing on our society, family, and nation. It was not a prayer promoting any particular religion or denomination. The Body of Christ was asleep and allowed one woman to change the course of our nation. A nation who's founding was on the principle of freedom of religion and not from religion. When a nation advocates the removal of God and its dependence on Him, then it has positioned itself in opposition to the Lord.

> *"Blessed is the nation whose God is the Lord, the people He has chosen as His heritage." Psalm 33:12*

With the removal of prayer from our schools, we now have a generation with scholastic scores well below average. Crime has incrementally increased at all levels. The door was opened for the introduction of another gospel to fill the void; the doctrine of secular humanism. Humanism is a man-centered doctrine rather than a God-centered theology. From the schoolhouse to the White House, we have witnessed abuses of power, blatant disregard for authority and for human life. Our politicians are adept at lying while kissing babies. They heap upon themselves wealth, power, and influence. The majority of our politicians no longer represent their constituents. Our prisons are overcrowded. There is a high recidivism rate among released felons. Society has no answer to all its ills. The divorce rate has skyrocketed since prayer was removed from our schools. There are more single-parent households than at any time in our nation's history. Our children are taught they are akin to animals and they, like animals, live by instinct. We don't teach self-control, instead condoms and birth control pills are dispensed to them. Our society is moving further and further from God's precepts. We are witnesses to laws being overturned and new ones legalizing homosexual marriages. We see the homosexual agenda implemented in our school system at the earliest ages possible. The indoctrination of the next generation is well underway. All while the church has hit the mute button on her voice. The Body of Christ must find her voice again. We must be silent no more. We need to beseech our Lord with prayer and fasting.

> *"If My people who are called by My name will humble themselves, and pray and seek My face, and turn from their wicked ways, then I will hear from heaven, and forgive their sin and heal their land." 2 Chronicles 7:14*

This is a very important passage on intercessory prayer. It teaches God's people that when there are problems in their nation, communities, families, and personal lives, God will heal those situations if they will come to Him in humility and repentance. This prayer teaches us that if God's conditions are met, which are we humble ourselves and turn away from our sin, He will hear, forgive our sins, and heal our land. This prayer is of vital importance concerning what is happening in most nations, communities, and homes in the world. Violence, drugs, alcoholism, crime, divorce, sexual perversion, economic problems, poverty, and disease are rampant in our world. However, God's people can do something about it if we humble ourselves in prayer and turn from our sin, expecting God to do what only He can (Spirit Life Bible).

When we look at the life of Jesus, we constantly see Him getting away to be alone to pray. Sometimes He prayed all night. He did nothing without first praying. It was in those times of prayer the Father revealed to Him what His next assignment was. If Jesus needed to receive revelation from God, then we surely need it. Without an active, vibrant, consistent prayer life, living this life will be next to impossible. Prayer is as essential to our life as water is to our physical bodies. When we are born again, we are no longer simply humans (Adamites) but a new race of supernatural beings called Christians. We are not merely humans; we are supernatural sons and daughters of the Most High God, filled with His Spirit and anointed to rule (Sheets, *Authority in Prayer*). Through prayer based on God's Word, God's anointing is released to break yokes and release the promises of God. Prayer changes things and people.

In the previous chapter, we talked about the words of our mouth. It is essential that our words line up with God's Word. We need to pray His Word over every situation and relationship. God has obligated Himself to remember His Word and to cause it to come to pass. There is a guarantee on His Word. He did not guarantee my word or your word. Therefore, with God's guarantee on His Word, then we can and should pray with absolute confidence.

> *"Put Me in remembrance: let us contend together: state your case, that you may be acquitted." Isaiah 43:26*

> *"For My thoughts are not your thoughts, nor are your ways My ways says the Lord. For as the heavens are higher than the earth, so are My ways higher than your ways, and My thoughts than your thoughts. For as the rain comes down, and snow from heaven, and do not return there, but water the earth, and make it bring forth and bud, that it may give seed to the sower and bread to the eater, So shall My Word be that goes forth from My mouth. It shall not return to Me void or empty. But it shall accomplish what I please, and it shall prosper in the thing for which I sent it."*
> *Isaiah 55: 8–11*

It's time for the Body of Christ to get back to the basics of Christianity. We are called to pray, give, and fast. Prayer for the believer should be a normal daily function. Notice I said for the believer. I did not say for pastors and leaders. All of us should be engaging in prayer as part of our daily routine. If you ain't praying, then you are not affecting change in your communities, families, and nation. If you ain't praying, you certainly are not laboring with the Lord. If you ain't praying, you have abandoned your basic responsibility as a believer. If you ain't praying, then our adversary has you right where he wants you. You pose no threat to his plans or his kingdom. If you ain't praying, the captives are still in captivity. If you ain't praying, you cannot complain when things are not changing.

Beloved, if you have been lulled into apathy in your prayer life, or lack thereof, repent and get back with the program. The Lord has a good plan for you. The Lord is gracious and merciful. God has an awesome plan laid out for each one of us long before the foundations of the world. It is not a plan of failure, misery, poverty, sickness, disaster, and disease. God's plan is a plan for life and health, happiness and fulfillment.

> *"For I know the thoughts and plans that I have for you, says the Lord, thoughts and plans for welfare and peace and for evil, to give you hope in your final outcome." Jeremiah 29:11*

> *"Beloved, I pray that you may prosper in every way and that your body may keep well, even as your soul keeps well and prospers." 3 John 2*

What shall be our legacy? Will it be one of indifference and apathy? Or will it be of seeing a wrong and endeavoring to make it right? There is a great cloud of witnesses looking over the balcony of heaven. They are cheering us on. To whom much is given, much is required. We cannot afford to waste one minute more. We have already allowed too much time to elapse. The Body of Christ must awake from her slumber and get on with our Father's business.

Let it be said of our generation that we are the generation that humbled themselves and repented for the sins of their nation. As a result of our intercession, the Lord rescued our generation and the generations to come. Should Jesus tarry, we shall witness the greatest harvest of souls ever. But we must pray and pray continually for God's will to be done on earth as it is in heaven.

"The righteous are bold as a lion."

CHAPTER 4

WHEN LAMBS BECOME LIONS

If we intend to succeed at being ourselves and truly enjoy our lives, we must allow the Holy Spirit to lead us. Only God, through His Spirit, can lead us to succeed and be all we can be. Being led by the Holy Spirit does not mean we never make mistakes. The Holy Spirit does not make mistakes, but we do. Following the Spirit's leading is a process that can be learned by doing. We start by stepping out into things we believe God is putting in our hearts, and we learn by wisdom and experience how to hear more clearly and definitely. It takes boldness to be led by the Spirit. It takes boldness to step out and boldness to survive when mistakes are made. We must remember that the righteous are bold as lions.

We must not forget who we are in Christ. We are in Him. In Christ, we also were made God's heritage, and we obtained an inheritance; for we have been foreordained in accordance with His purpose. Our identity is in Christ. Every believer of Jesus Christ is a citizen of heaven and member of the household of God. You are now a member of God's own household! With Jesus Christ as the chief cornerstone, we are being made part of a holy temple for the dwelling place of God in the Spirit. When you begin to understand who you are in Christ and the totally incredible thing God is doing in your life, you will never again be confused about your identity.

As I said in the beginning of this book, we are identified by a variety of names by the Lord. Just like our Lord Jesus who was the Lamb of God, we too are identified as lambs and sheep.

> *Jesus said, "I am the door of the sheep. All who ever came before Me are thieves and robbers, but the sheep did not hear them. The thief does not come except to steal, and to kill, and to destroy. I have come that they may have life and that may have it more abundantly. I am the good shepherd. The good shepherd gives His life for the sheep. I am the good shepherd and I know MY sheep and am known by My own." John 10:7–8, 10–11, 14*

Believers are similar to sheep that need a shepherd to lead and protect them. Like sheep, believers are to recognize the voice of their true Shepherd. This implies that there are other voices to which believers should not listen. There is a thief and robber whose objective is to lead the sheep astray. Nevertheless, sheep that learn to recognize the voice of their Shepherd will not be led astray by false prophets, false doctrines, and false messiahs. To hear God and avoid the spirit of error, it's important to look into God's Word and spend time with Him. The more we study and learn, the more we become rooted and grounded in Him. The Lord wants us to be so acquainted with Him and His Word, when other voices speak, we will quickly discern the Master's voice.

In the banking industry, clerks study real money. They become experts in identifying the genuine so when counterfeit bills are passed, they are easily detected. That is how we should be with the Word of God and hearing His voice. Time spent with the Lord is crucial. Jesus said, "My sheep will know My voice." As we spend time with Him, He will give us discernment to know if what we are hearing is truly from Him or not. This facet of our life is paramount. We live in a time where the voices are many. Much of what we hear sounds like God but is not God.

Satan has one goal, and that is destruction. He comes only to kill, steal, and destroy everything good that God has in mind for us. He knows his time is short. We must make every day count for the glory of God. Now is the time for us to rise up as lions and roar against the works of darkness. The righteous are bold as lions. We have a mandate from our Lord to go into all the world and preach the gospel, cast out devils, and heal the sick. No time for whimpering.

> "Then one of the elders said to me, Stop weeping! See, the Lion of the tribe of Judah has won, has overcome and conquered." Revelation 5:5

Earlier we talked about some of the characteristics of lambs and sheep. Let us look at a few traits of lions. Lions are protective. They protect territory, their young and themselves. Lions are brave and courageous. They don't shy away from predators. The bravery of lions has earned them title as king of the jungle. They are willing to fight. The Body of Christ will have to adopt lion-like characteristics. We must be relentless and unrelenting against the kingdom of darkness.

The characteristics of the lion are totally different from those of the lamb, yet the Lord is recognized as having both qualities. Throughout the gospels, Jesus seems to act in two contrasting ways. He confronts the money changers in the temple with iron-like intensity, overthrowing their tables and firmly demonstrating God's will to all those who watched Him. Yet in other places, we see Jesus as a lamb, standing falsely accused without speaking one word in His own defense.

> *"He was oppressed, yet when He was afflicted, He was submissive and opened not His mouth; like a lamb that is led to the slaughter, and as sheep before her shearers is dumb, so He opened not His mouth." Isaiah 53:7*

Beloved, time has come for us to be counted and heard. We have the good news of the gospel to proclaim to a dying world. We must come together in unity to advance the kingdom of God. We must stop being offended with one another. We should live a life of forgiving one another often and always. We cannot hold on to things that are opposed to the will of God. If you don't know what His will is, then go to His book. Beloved, stand up for righteousness in our churches, our homes, our communities, our workplaces, and our nation. We are called in this hour to roar against darkness, against injustice, against all that opposes the Word of God. Those who are friends with the world are enemies of God.

> *"You are like unfaithful wives having illicit love affairs with the world and breaking your marriage vow to God. Do you not know that being the world's friend is being God's enemy? So whoever chooses to stand be a friend of the world takes his stand as an enemy of God." James 4:4*

The Lord is calling His people back to holiness, back to Himself. Awake unto righteousness, says the scripture. Wake up, church. Time has come for the Body of Christ to judge herself and repent for her complacency, her love affair with the world, and her indifference to those who are lost without Christ in this world. We must regain focus of our mission here on earth. When God gives the church in a city the right order of government and gifting, when the church begins to come into proper order, we then have the authority to dethrone the thrones of iniquity that rule in our cities. Under the new covenant, the Lord has given us access through His Spirit to dismantle the things in the heavens that are holding back His inheritance for a territory. We are to war with the powers and principalities that are withholding blessings (Ahn, *The Reformer's Pledge*).

As new creations we are fully equipped to live a victorious life. Even though we are saved by grace with forgiveness of sin we will have to give an account for everything we have said and done with our lives. God has given us the gift of life, and He wants us to partner with Him in making our lives count for the kingdom. Be faithful to Him.

> *"Therefore do not cast away your confidence which has great reward. For you have need of endurance, so that after you have done the will of God, you may receive the promise." Hebrews 10:35–36*

The marines used to have a slogan: *"When the going gets tough, the tough get going."* Nowhere in scripture does it promise smooth sailing for God's people. It does say, however, there will be persecutions and tribulations, but we are to have good courage because our Lord is ever with us. His promise to us is that He will never leave us or forsake us. Even though we walk through the valley of the shadow of death, He is with us. Scripture says that we are to endure hardship like a good soldier.

> *"Take [with me] your share of the hardships and suffering, which you are called to endure, as a good (first class) soldier*

of Christ Jesus. No soldier when in service gets entangled in the enterprises of civilian life; his aim is to satisfy and please the one who enlisted him." 2 Timothy 2:3

I can identify with this passage because I served in the United States Navy for twenty-one years. The purpose of boot camp is to retrain, retool, and reshape individuals coming from civilian life. At the conclusion of the eight weeks of boot camp, there is clear evidence of a dramatic change in attitude, manner, walk, speech, and thinking. The process of reshaping is an intense time of drilling, marching, constant correction and teaching and, in some cases, punishment. The ultimate goal is to make every recruit fit for service. Are there hardships? Yes, there are. Is there suffering? Absolutely! By keeping one's eyes on the prize and knowing there's an expiration date, graduation, made it worth it. Similarly, when one gives his or her heart to Jesus, there is a time of intense training. The difference, however, is that our training in the kingdom of God is a lifetime of learning and growing. His training is designed to make us fit for the kingdom of God. As citizens of His kingdom, we learn how the kingdom operates. We learn who God is and what He is not. A transformation takes place as we yield ourselves to the Holy Spirit. We are trained so that we can go and do as He has commanded.

As the Body of Christ prepares herself to operate in the fullness of her calling, love will be at the center—love of God and love for others. We can do a million acts of kindness, but if we have not loved, it counts for nothing. We can wage a good warfare, but if we are not rooted and grounded in the love of God, it means nothing. The Body of Christ must mature in her love walk. Jesus said the world will know us by our love. Love must be front and center if we're ever going to win the unsaved.

The Lord is calling us to hear the heartbeat of the Father for the poor, the lost, and the broken. He is calling each one of us to care for His lost children. He is looking for willing vessels of love willing to give their lives away in service to Him and to others. I believe Jesus is raising up a whole army, a generation of radical, sold-out servant lovers armed and dangerous to the kingdom of darkness. I believe there is an army of believers who are not afraid to venture into the enemy's camp and free the captives. I believe our Lord is strategically positioning His people. Jesus said that we should occupy until He comes. He did not infer that we sit around and do nothing.

We are to conduct kingdom business until His return. We must rise up as lions and roar against all that oppose the will of God. It is time, little sheep, to don the mantle of the lion. For such a time as this we were created. We are called to advance the kingdom of our Lord Jesus Christ. All is not lost, Church! We have an opportunity to turn this around. Now faith is the substance of things hoped for, the evidence of things not seen. Stand behind the shield of faith and call those things which are not as though they were. Stand at the ready and believe! Because our God is bigger than anything the devil throws at us. Be men and women who are persistent in prayer, seeing the possibilities in God because all things are possible to them who believe. We are a people of faith.

Beloved, pray red-hot passionate prayers. Do not relent. The effectual, fervent prayer of a righteous man makes tremendous power available.

> "Rejoice always pray without ceasing; in everything give thanks; for this is God's will for you in Christ Jesus." 1 Thessalonians 5:16–18

God does not change. He wants to demonstrate His power in the church and through the church today just as He did in her beginning. As people of faith, we need to be praying for that to happen. We must not allow ourselves to be intimidated. Instead, keep our eyes on Jesus, the Source of our power and strength, the One who stands ready to confirm His Word through signs and wonders. We are to step out in faith and obedience to what He has called us to do. God has chosen to work through human vessels, and when we are willing to allow God to work through us, we open the door for great demonstrations of His power.

We are here for the express purpose of populating heaven and plundering hell. As occupation forces, we are to enforce the victory of Jesus by subduing kingdoms, dispelling darkness, bringing hope to the hopeless, and loving the masses. For that reason, I am not ashamed of the gospel of Jesus Christ, and I will not be silent. I will not be silent anymore! Time for us to do something. If not you then who?

The stage is set. Now is the time when lambs shall become lions. Roar, beloved, roar! And be silent no more, and be bold as lions! I conclude with words from a Julie Meyer worship song "Unto the Lamb."

> *"Unto the Lamb in the midst of the Throne. The beautiful Lamb in the midst of the Throne. The Worthy Lamb, The Glorious Man-Slain. I saw in the right hand of Him who sat on the Throne a scroll. Written on the inside and out and sealed with seven seals. I saw a strong angel proclaiming with a loud voice, Who is Worthy to take the Scroll and loose its seals? And there was no one in Heaven, nor on the earth or underneath. No one was found worthy and I began to weep. Then one of the Elders said to me, 'Do not weep, Behold. The Lion of the Tribe of Judah has prevailed.'"*

As He is, so are we in this world.

REFERENCES

Ahn, Che. 2012. *The Reformer's Pledge.* Shippensburg: Destiny Image Publishers.

Hamon, Bill. 1981. *The Eternal Church.* Shippensburg: Destiny Image Publishers.

Meyer, Julie. 2010. *God Is Alive.* Compact disc.

Morris, Robert. 2006. *The Power of Your Words.* Ventura: Regal Publishers.

Savelle, Jerry. 2012. *The Favor of God.* Ventura: Regal Publishers.

Sheets, Dutch. 2006. *Authority in Prayer.* Minneapolis: Bethany House.

Spurgeon, Charles Haddon. 1871. "The Sheep and Their Shepherd." Sermon presented at the Metropolitan Tabernacle.

Thomas Nelson. 1995. *Spirit-Filled Life Bible.* Thomas Nelson.

Zondervan and The Lockman Foundation. 1987. *The Amplified Bible.* Grand Rapids: Zondervan and The Lockman Foundation.

Johnson, Bill & Clark, Randy. 2011. *The Essential Gide to Healing. Minneapolis: Chosen Books.*

www.ingramcontent.com/pod-product-compliance
Lightning Source LLC
LaVergne TN
LVHW092056060526
838201LV00047B/1421